Radical Response

Free Market Solutions to Global Crises

By

Richard Lackey and Thom Garlock

Foreword by Walter Rakowich

Contents

About the Authors

Richard Lackey is the founder of the Global Food Exchange™, a for-profit company uniquely designed to provide benevolent and long-term sustainable solutions for the provision of critical post-disaster supplies.

A serial entrepreneur with a unique background that includes several years in emergency medical response and medical missions as well as almost three decades as an active trader and fund manager, Richard has appeared as an expert in the field in magazines, and on radio and television. He has held eight different securities licenses spanning equity, options and futures markets, and has served as the managing director for five private funds.

Richard's expertise in emergency response management and his perceptions of the inefficiencies of disaster response led him to join with a world-class team of experts to create the Global Food Exchange™. The goal of the Global Food Exchange™ is to establish the world's most valuable commodities as the world's newest and potentially safest asset class. Richard is also passionate about utilizing the Global Food Exchange™ as a solution for the inefficiencies that have existed in getting critical supplies to disaster victims.

Richard has authored three books on technical analysis and investment management and regularly consults with startup companies needing innovative solutions, marketing direction, or board leadership.

Richard spends as much time as possible with his wife of twenty years and his two beautiful daughters hiking, biking, and traveling the globe.

Thom Garlock is the founder of the WorldFoodCrusade.org, a non-profit enterprise focused on providing food to victims of natural disasters, as well as educating consumers on issues related to food security and non-sustainable food production methods in use today. He is also an introducing agent of the Global Food Exchange™.

Since 1985, Thom has been active as a real estate investor and developer in the Jackson Hole, Wyoming and Southern California regions. He is the managing partner of Teton Land & Development Group, LLC, a real estate development company that currently creates master planned communities in Wyoming and Idaho.

In the 1980s, Thom was fortunate to be an early pioneer in the cellular telephone industry as a principal in a variety of wireless communications license-based ventures that have held and developed over fifty metropolitan area cellular telephone licenses throughout the United States.

Thom has presented his research on investing in tangible assets at numerous wealth conferences and has appeared on America's Premier Experts® TV show on ABC, CBS, NBC, and Fox.

Acknowledgements

While it is common place for authors to produce a litany of names and references to those who have inspired us, directed us, or just put up with us, the most important person we must acknowledge in this effort is clearly you, the reader, for whom we hope this book will incite to action. We hope that you will share the challenge with others, to empower the less fortunate with the truly sustainable solutions that come from systems built on free market principles.

For those who have incited us to action, we are forever in your debt. The team at the Global Food Exchange that have supported this effort directly; Jason Aubrey, our Managing Director, and Matthew Biegner, our Communications Director, and our world class Board of Managers and Advisors, you guys are the best. Others who helped build the model of operations of GFE, like Jami Garvais, or folks like Norton Rainey, Jane Norton, and Jonathan Thomas, who helped take GFE to many of the world's great influencers, we are forever thankful. Duane Reed, advisor and friend, and his awesome wife Kay deserve a big thank you for your input and for keeping this effort on track.

Thom and I both agree that our best investment has been time spent with our families. Thom's beautiful wife Karen and my lovely wife Paige are as driven and passionate about making the world a better place as any that we know. That is what inspires us to do more and to do better. My daughters, Sydney and Ansley, may have summed it up best when they said that their time spent with others exploring life's challenges makes them part of each other's story. We know everyone has a great story, and we appreciate you allowing us to share a bit of ours.

Foreword

I have always been in awe of the entrepreneurs of this world who have discovered creative ways to solve a problem and earn money for themselves and others by delivering a product or service. Some of these solutions are so profound as to save the lives of people and animals, while others are more convenience oriented (toward improving the quality of life), and still others are just fads that distract us from the day-to-day mundane. All entrepreneurs have one thing in common; a vision.

The vision of the entrepreneurial authors of this book is to create a solution which will potentially save the lives of millions of people, and I am honored to have been asked to write this foreword. One has to ask why this life-saving solution has not been implemented before now. I am guessing, many of you already thought it was. I know I did.

As a former CEO of an international corporation I experienced first-hand how the private sector is in a great position to help solve many of the world's problems because in many cases they have the expertise, the financial and people resources and a genuine desire to make a difference in their communities. Companies do not even need to be in the business of solving a particular issue; they just need to think creatively and be proactive, and know that they often have much to offer given their influence and what they bring to the table. I saw this while running Prologis.

Prologis is the world's largest owner of warehouses in the world; and even with our obvious size and geographic diversity, we wondered at one point in time how a company that was a niche real estate owner could make a difference. We realized that some of those warehouses could be used in disaster relief efforts to house supplies for disasters like the earthquake in Haiti. In that case, we had a product advantage that could be used as a solution for the Red Cross. We also realized that we had construction expertise and relationships that could help in building schools in China. We brought local resources together to help solve a local issue in that country, where we were growing rapidly. And, in doing these things, we found that our employees engaged like never before because we had a purpose which extended far beyond our day-to-day business. These efforts were win-win solutions because we were able to use what we had to solve local problems in the communities in which we operated; we were able to genuinely engage our employees in activities that they felt great about; and we were able to build a positive brand image for our business throughout the world and, more importantly, support the residents of these local communities in a time of need.

While Prologis has joined a growing consortium of global companies weaving social benevolence into the fabric of their organization, there are new organizations popping up that have literally integrated "doing well by doing good" into the design and infrastructure of their companies. Even third world countries, who have historically been in need of our donations, are now asking that the continued stream of donations stop, and the focus be re-directed to helping in the creation of jobs. It's clearly not just corporations that are innovating. The trend among many of the world's largest non-profits is the coordination of expertise, including business leaders and educators, to promote business as an integral part of their mission. From an economic standpoint, free markets are the proven champions for overcoming poverty and creating prosperous societies. As the authors explain so well, all boats rise with the tide where markets grow. The benefits of free markets provide both short-term relief and true long-term economic sustainability.

Of course, we all inherently want to provide for our families and ourselves. We also have that innate desire to ensure that our children have more opportunities for a future as good as or better than our own. Improving economic security from one generation to the next is largely a result of having established systems in place for access to education and by some measure, to markets. Being dependent on government and others may have some value in the short run, but in the long run, dependency creates an anemia in those societies, which become victims of this largesse. As creative systems, markets and exchanges like those shared in Radical Response become more commonplace, we may very well see an incredible global betterment. The authors of Radical Response share ideas that should be considered an invitation to open the dialogue on free market solutions to global crises and other great social challenges.

I invite and encourage you to read this book and to share it with others. By nature, we have always wanted to help our fellow man when we can. Richard and Thom have created an amazing vehicle to help all of us help save the lives of others through an incredible "exchange". But, I want you to also know that Radical Response is much more than that. This book explains that the necessary shift is not just in the creation, design and development of products, but in creating and executing world-wide sustainable systems. Upon reading the introduction I better understood the worldly problem and couldn't wait to read the book to learn the solution. I found Radical Response to be one of the best non-fiction books I've read. I think you will too.

Walter Rakowich

Mr. Rakowich is a former CEO of Prologis, where he worked for 18 years before retiring in December 2012.

Preface

There is just no reason for millions to die, or for hundreds of millions more to suffer needlessly, when the solutions are at our fingertips. While we now have more technology on this planet than ever in history, we have an equally incredible measure of affliction, and it just doesn't add up.

Throughout my life, whether in emergency medicine or fund management, I have always had a passion for finding and resolving inefficiencies. For many years I found great rewards in the inefficiencies of the financial markets, which were abundant, regardless of what many "efficient market" professors suggest. As time progressed, I realized a multitude of challenges that face our world today can be minimized or even eliminated through the use of innovative business models, using what I would call "business model arbitrage." The most compelling opportunities can be found in the interconnecting of modern for-profit and traditional not-for-profit business models to dramatically improve both the efficiency and sustainability of a benevolent mission. Adam Smith, the eighteenth-century economist often referred to as the father of economics, suggested that the butcher does not sell his meats because his primary goal is to feed others, but to feed his own family. The production of food for his friends and neighbors is secondary or even incidental to his desire to provide for his family.

That being said, it is imperative that the butcher seek out the specific needs of his prospective clients so that he might be competitive in the marketplace. The "invisible hand" of competition should then guide the butcher to adjust the quality of service and the cost of products to maximize income.

As the social fabric of First World countries grows threadbare, and long suffering countries desperately seek real measures for achieving the hope and prosperity of First World countries, the greatest need is for business models or systems that can bridge the gap in a multitude of circumstances. We would suggest a business model that would reflect the influence of the 'benevolent hand', whereby business is organized for the purpose of resolving a social problem with a free market solution, thus making the system truly sustainable. This concept, derived in part from a focus on building systems rather than products, seems to resonate with government leaders, business leaders and entrepreneurs alike.

Craig Fugate, FEMA Administrator, at a recent DHS-FEMA conference on Building Resiliency through Public-Private Partnership made a great point when he shared his view that (to paraphrase) regardless of your political leanings, whether you believe government should do more to solve problems or that government should stop inserting itself in so many areas, the simple truth is that government cannot do it all.

In the United States, our ability to manage the response to disasters has improved dramatically, largely from efforts directed at bringing together disparate resources, including government and non-government agencies as well as the private sector. Whether intended or not, the most powerful and effective efforts have resulted in systems that allow for improvements over time as more participants join the effort.

There is, however, a distinct difference in the systems created by government and those created by profit seeking entities. Those that are profit seeking have a natural predilection toward efficiency, as inefficiency reduces the potential viability of the company; while governments, especially those that can print their own money, have less motivation to seek efficiency.

A movement in the non-profit world has driven non-profit organizations to fund programs that are more effective and to provide higher levels of accountability and transparency to their donors. Organizations like Charity Watch and Charity Navigator have become popular resources for donors wanting to make sure their dollars are being used effectively. They employ common financial analysis tools to standardize operational efficiencies so that prospective donors might evaluate each organization on similar footing. For the majority of large donors who have built their net worth operating companies, the ability to self-select four-star organizations, like Samaritan's Purse on a national basis or Colorado-based ACE Scholarships on the local-level, precipitates consistently stronger investments while spurring lesser-rated organizations to improve performance, much like a publicly traded stock company.

In a trend running almost parallel to this is that of companies influenced by the benevolent hand. Driven by an emerging desire to change the world for the better,

12

entrepreneurs are now seeking to solve the world's most dire problems by fusing entrepreneurial innovation and creativity with social benevolence to establish incredible new systems.

For those who readily recognize the innumerable inefficiencies in the world today, it comes as no surprise that there are some much larger and tragic consequences to a great many of these if they are continually left unresolved. So, how do we best leverage mission, skills, and innovative business design for truly radical results? The answers are to be found in the systematic cross-pollination of free market experts with those who are already vested in the process. We will highlight several examples, including our own Global Food Exchange™, which required the collaborative efforts of manufacturers, logistic experts, investment and distribution companies, as well as government and non-governmental organizations to create a dependable solution for getting food and other resources to post-disaster sites faster than ever before.

Clearly, the solutions built on free market principles with express designs promoting a benevolent purpose have some distinct advantages in the market place. We will highlight the advantages as well as some of the challenges and potential disadvantages, but we believe the evidence is overwhelmingly in support of a new approach; a call to a more radical entrepreneurial approach to resolving global crises that should greatly enhance and even leverage the effectiveness of philanthropy.

Richard L. Lackey

Introduction

"We have seven days to save them," said Marine Corp Brigadier General Paul Kennedy in his initial report following the devastating Typhoon Haiyan. The storm literally changed the landscape of the Philippines.

Three days later, we witnessed a mother leaving the ruins of a building with one child after having entered with three. Upon further query, we found that this young mother had no food left, and with all of them suffering the effects of contaminated water she was hoping to save the oldest and strongest. She was forced to make the decision to leave her one year old and two year old to die. We wondered, if this was what happened after three days what would this place be like in seven days?

Such tragic scenes are not new; these and many more have been a part of the human experience for thousands of years. Since the dawn of time human life has been precarious, and in many ways it still is. Every day, and in endless varieties, environmental afflictions beset us.

Ancient writings tell of floods and earthquakes and volcanoes, and of famine and pestilence. An Egyptian relief found on the causeway of the Fifth Dynasty Pyramid of Unas in Sakkara tells of the earliest recorded famine. It happened about 2500 BCE, when the entire population of the earth was only about twenty million people. This is roughly equal to the current population of the state of Florida.

Somehow these ancient peoples survived and even thrived. By the time of Jesus, the world population had managed to grow to about two hundred million, but these were short lives, each with an average duration of thirty years. When the Black Death struck in the middle of the fourteenth century, the human population declined from 440 million to 350 million. In a few short, devastating years we lost over a century of population growth! But by the year 1500 we had made up the losses, and as the nineteenth century dawned we reached the first big milestone: one billion people.

As our numbers increased we began to worry not about our extinction but whether the earth could sustain its burgeoning human population. In 1798, the Reverend Thomas Robert

Malthus published *An Essay on the Principle of Population* in which he asserted that population growth would be checked by famine and disease. In opposition to the popular view in eighteenth-century Europe that saw society both steadily improving and perfectible, Malthus proposed that the consequences of population growth precluded progress towards a utopian society: "The power of population is indefinitely greater than the power in the earth to produce subsistence for man."

Despite his predictions, and despite floods, droughts, and famine, by 1930 the global population reached two billion. Our growth accelerated, and we quickly added billions upon billions more to our numbers.

Today we number seven billion souls. And, when compared to the Middle Ages, it's not just the number of people but the number of *people years* that has multiplied: today the average human life expectancy is sixty-seven, more than twice as long as a person living in the days of King Arthur. We are not only more numerous, but in addition we each require a steady supply of food and water for many more years than our predecessors did.

To the credit of the human race, with some notable exceptions we've done our best to alleviate the horrors of what our environment can do to us. Ancient Egyptians stockpiled grain to provide food during those seasons when the life-giving Nile didn't flood the fields. The Romans built aqueducts to carry water to their cities. The native people of the Americas designed sturdy portable shelters that could be easily transported across the vast prairies to follow the herds of migrating bison. The Dutch built windmills to capture wind energy that could grind grain.

Creating and implementing these solutions requires methods of evaluation and distribution. Not all ideas are good ones. In the days of Rome, carrying water in pipes was a good idea. Making the pipes out of lead was a bad idea. Ideas need to be brought to the marketplace, tested, refined, tested again, and endlessly perfected. Ideas must respond to changing conditions. The concept that seemed to work well yesterday may not work today.

Disaster relief—the rushing of life-saving aid to victims of flood, storm, or drought—has most often been the responsibility of either governments or charitable non-governmental organizations (NGOs). As this book will reveal, history will show that the results have been mixed. Sometimes the challenges are bigger than expected; sometimes the intentions are good but the results disappointing; and sometimes authoritarian governments even allow their citizens to suffer.

Radical Response confronts the problem of human survival through a bold new perspective. Authors Richard Lackey and Thom Garlock carefully survey the landscape of disaster relief, weigh the pros and cons of traditional approaches, and take stock of new technologies that are available to us for the first time in our history. When considered together, these factors have led the authors to an exciting new possibility for bringing aid to suffering populations. It's a model based on the free market system, where capitalist actors create, fund, and then deploy life-saving food, energy, water, and temporary shelter systems to any part of the globe that has experienced a life-threatening natural or man-made disaster. While some of the technologies may impact the bigger picture, these are not intended to be long-term solutions to chronic drought, famine, or homelessness. Instead, they're intended to save lives that are immediately imperiled, during such times when decisive action must be taken within days and even hours.

In the first chapter, the book surveys the vast and varied scope of both natural and man-made disasters that relentlessly plague humanity. These include water shortages, climate volatility, earthquakes, electrical blackouts, volcanic eruptions, and violent storms. These problems—the natural ones, at least—have been with us since the dawn of time, and show no sign of ending.

The second chapter looks at solutions that have been carried out by governments. This chapter is not intended to criticize dedicated public servants but rather to highlight the challenges inherent in formulating and carrying out a well-intentioned government-led relief effort. Of course some governments are unfortunately venal, and abuse their own citizens; these are easy targets and the records of their wrongdoings would fill endless volumes. Such governments are touched upon here, but are not the primary focus of the book.

The third chapter introduces the concept that a new path is open for disaster relief: the power of the free market system. Unlike charity, which is a one-way action in which the giving party expects no material benefit from the exchange, the free market system is built upon the idea that humans are powerfully motivated when they enter into an exchange in which all parties benefit. When compared to a government effort, a disaster relief program that is based on a free market model and funded by investors may be considered to be more transparent, less prone to waste, quicker to respond, and better able to adapt itself to changing conditions.

Chapter four introduces a specific program that follows this free market model: the Global Food Exchange™ (GFE). This innovative investment concept takes the very best ideas in food, energy, water, and shelter technology and combines them with the powerful motivating force of the free market system. The result is a set of dynamic real-world solutions that have the potential to transform disaster relief and save lives.

The fifth chapter looks ahead at what we can expect in the future: a growing world population, a flattening of agricultural and livestock production, and steadily rising food prices. This is not a doomsday scenario, just common sense. There is no doubt that humans will figure out how to meet these challenges, and there is also no doubt that the solutions will require imagination and the willingness to think outside of traditional ideas.

Through the implementation of new ideas we humans have survived on our fragile spinning rock, and that is how we can expect to create a bright future for generations to come.

Chapter One: The Challenges of Humanity

In a small coastal town a family surveys the shattered remains of their house. The violent storm and flood had come quickly, leaving them little time to escape with a few belongings. Having passed the night at an inland shelter, the mother and father and their three children are physically safe. But now life has taken on a harsh new reality. They have no insurance; no bank account. The father's job as a laborer earns the family a few dollars a day. He's not sure he even has a job any more. The children are hungry and the family's meager supply of rice has been ruined by sewage from the floodwaters. They do not know where to turn for help because all of their neighbors are in the same situation. The mayor of the town has no answers. The federal government has pledged assistance but the father and mother have seen no one and have no idea where to go.

Far away, on another part of the globe, a family stands in the middle of their barren field. The drought has lasted months now, and the rainy season has not arrived. There is no water to grow maize, or much of anything else for that matter. Near the dried-up lake there's a water pump that the government installed years ago, but it doesn't work and no one knows how to fix it. There's no grass for the three cows, whose ribs are showing. To avoid starvation the family will have to sell the cows for a pittance, which means that when the rains finally come, the family will have to buy new cows. They have no other wealth. The mother pounds the last bits of millet and wonders how she's going to get more. The children will have to go to work as beggars or, for the daughter, perhaps something even worse. The father hurries into the house and says that he has heard about a water truck coming to the next town. It's a two-hour walk. He's leaving now because if he's late the water will be gone.

On another continent, across the ocean, a family picks itself up after a violent earthquake. The town has been virtually destroyed. From under the debris you can hear the cries of the injured. The family's house is nothing but rubble. Their car has been crushed by a falling wall. In the air is the pungent smell of gas. The father and mother have no time to ponder their predicament. They need to get their kids to safety and find them some food and clean water. In a bank account they have some money, but the neighborhood ATM has been destroyed and the bank branch is across town. They cannot wait for people in faraway offices to have meetings and issue directives. They need help now.

The scenes described above are neither unique nor, sadly, uncommon. As they have since the dawn of time, disasters strike with sad regularity. Hurricanes rage, earthquakes shake the ground, volcanoes erupt, droughts turn farmland into desert. It's the way of the world.

It's not going to change. We live in a universe not of predictability and stasis, but of uncertainty and risk. From uncertainty and risk come both progress and calamity. Progress results from our attempts to improve our lives and reduce risk. Calamities are caused by two things: the actions of nature and the imperfections of man. Natural calamities come simply because that's how the universe operates. The world does what it does without regard to our desires or expectations. We try to control our environment, but our efforts are never perfectly successful. Despite the breathtaking technological progress that humans have made over the past fifteen thousand years—indeed, in the past century alone—we have not been able to erase hardship and affliction from the human experience. All over the world, every hour of every day, human beings are battered by natural forces that create poverty, illness, and needless death.

We are also victims of calamities of our own making. Some are simply terrible mistakes, such as when a great ocean liner strikes an iceberg and sinks. But many are the result of greed and ignorance. Too often humans pursue agendas and ideologies—religious, political, economic—that, when seen from the objective vantage point of history, are patently and obviously wrong. Thirty-five years after the fall of the Berlin Wall, who among us cannot see why the rigid state-controlled economy of the Soviet Union was doomed to collapse? Who cannot see today that the dictatorship of North Korea will never be capable of bringing prosperity to that wretched country? Is it no surprise that a nation like Ireland became a thriving economy only after decades of terrible sectarian violence was put aside in favor of unity and cooperation?

Taken together, the number and variety of afflictions that shorten the lives of humans range from powerful nuclear bombs and earthquakes to microscopic bacteria and viruses. They include every conceivable variety of man-made and natural threat. Some disasters wipe out millions of people in minutes, while others spread slowly and take one life at a time.

These calamities are far too numerous and varied to be catalogued in one book. As a practical matter, this book will present a representative survey in four key areas: food, water, shelter, and energy. We will not include other areas such as medicine and criminal law, but common sense suggests that scenarios overlap among every area of affliction. One chapter will present a special focus on food inequity.

The goal of this book is to demonstrate that throughout human history, and particularly in the modern era, the free market system has consistently produced advances in the overall standard of living for billions of people, and has outperformed competing economic systems including socialism and other forms of direct government control. While government provides certain services, like a common defense and the enforcement of law, in a manner made efficient by its size and by the congruous concession of a participating citizenry, government in many other instances tends to be unfocused, illogical, and driven by conflicting values. The free markets are more tightly focused, based on logic, and motivated by values that are clear and simple. Governments are concerned with nationalism, while free markets strive to break down artificial national boundaries that impede progress. As we face both new and familiar challenges in the years and even centuries to come, there can be no doubt that the unfettered ingenuity of men and women working in the free enterprise system will continue to produce the astonishing progress that we have witnessed and experienced in our lifetimes.

It is anticipated that there will be readers who, having read these first few paragraphs, will throw up their hands and announce that the history of the world is full of examples of both greedy free market corporations and benevolent central governments. This is true. During every era and on every continent, we can find plenty of examples of both. We've all read about terrible pollution caused by a factory, or shareholders swindled by a corrupt board of directors, or hapless consumers duped by shoddy products. We've also read about, or have experienced, many of the good things that governments have done to benefit their citizens. When your house is on fire, a government-sponsored fire department will put out the blaze. If you are mugged, the government-paid police officer will come to your aid. You may have attended a public school or state university. Your health may have been enhanced by government-funded research into the causes of disease.

The many examples of both positive results obtained by government and negative results obtained by private enterprise do not change the great weight of evidence that has accumulated over centuries: When people are free to pursue solutions to humanity's problems, without being encumbered by either ideology or a preconceived theory of philosophical correctness, forward progress is made. In the private sector, success is clearly rewarded, while failure—without which there can be no progress—is often limited to the risk assumed by the owners and participants in the venture. In bureaucratic central governments, the wrong kind of success is often rewarded, and failure is either catastrophic or swept under the rug.

To build the foundation for the argument that free enterprise has been and will continue to be the brightest hope for humanity, let's first take a survey of a few of the many challenges facing human beings, as represented by both natural and man-made disasters.

Water Shortages in Latin America

The seriousness of the current world water crisis has been well documented. In all parts of the globe over one billion people are without access to safe water, and it is estimated that nearly two million children die every year because they don't have access to an adequate supply of clean water.

You might assume that we're talking about people who live in deserts. Sadly, this is not the case.

With the most annual rainfall of any region in the world, Latin America is experiencing a water crisis. Too many residents of the region turn on their taps only to have nothing come out. Yet water abounds, at least in terms of scientific measurement. Despite the seeming abundance of fresh water, a 2006 World Bank study shows average water bills in Latin America are the highest of all regions in the developing world. Latin America has one of the most inequitable income distribution rates in the world, with one result being that water access in the region is also inequitable.

In 2006, the United Nations Development Program (UNDP) issued a report entitled "Why There's a Water Crisis in the Most Water-Rich Region." The report stated, "The scarcity at the heart of the global water crisis is rooted in power, poverty and inequality, not in physical availability."

21

Water inequity isn't the only challenge. Since the latter part of the twentieth century, the Central American region has seen a substantial increase in the number of natural disasters. Weather conditions are expected to become even more erratic, including droughts caused by the El Niño phenomenon.

When inflation, rising food prices, and unstable weather are combined, food shortages and under-nutrition are the results.

The regional bureau for Latin America and the Caribbean has indicated that more than fifty-two million people—nine million of whom are children under the age of five—are marginalized by chronic under-nutrition. Anemia is the most widespread nutritional issue in the region and affects millions of preschool children and women of childbearing age. Recurrent natural disasters, high food prices, and the global economic downturn further exacerbate the vulnerability of at-risk populations in the area.

A long-term project that began in January 2011 will focus on a school feeding program. The expected outcome of the project is to increase sustainability and quality of the national school feeding programs in the twelve-country area. These countries include Bolivia, Columbia, Cuba, Ecuador, El Salvador, Guatemala, Haiti, Honduras, Nicaragua, and Peru.

Too much water can be as damaging as too little. The United States Agency for International Development (US AID) reported that in October 2011, for nine days Tropical Depression 12-E—a massive tropical cyclone in the Pacific Ocean—produced huge amounts of rain in Guatemala, El Salvador, Honduras and Nicaragua. With rainfall amounts for the first two weeks of the month already above expected rainfall totals for the month, crops and infrastructure were damaged and hundreds of thousands of people were displaced. At least ninety-three deaths were reported as a result of the flooding and over one hundred thousand people were evacuated. Bean, corn, coffee, and sugar crops were severely affected.

There is nothing that humans can do about cyclones and hurricanes, but we can prepare in advance for their damaging effects. With appropriate resources in place to quickly provide shelter, water, food, and energy, local populations can rebound much more readily, and before secondary effects, such as disease, have a chance to take hold.

The Texas Drought

The Texas drought began in October 2010 and has continued through the time of this writing. For three years, most of the state has experienced severe rainfall shortages. Experts have warned that Texas could be in the midst of a drought worse than the last major drought of record during the 1950s. No single year during that drought was as dry as 2011 was, with an average of only 14.8 inches of rain. The high temperatures over the summer months increased evaporation, further lowering river and lake levels. The state experienced a short and rainy respite in the winter and spring of 2012, but by the fall of 2012 arid conditions had returned to most of the state.

As of this writing, ninety-five percent of Texas is in some form of drought conditions, and the state's reservoirs are less than seventy percent full. The state climatologist predicted abnormally dry weather and higher than average temperatures through summer 2013, which could make the drought worse than the drought of record in the 1950s. About sixteen percent of the state is in what experts call "exceptional" drought, the worst stage.

Why is there a drought in Texas? The primary cause of the intense 2011 dryness was La Niña, a weather pattern where the surface temperatures are cooler in the Pacific. This in turn creates drier, warmer weather in the southern United States. La Niña lingers for a year, sometimes longer, and tends to return once every few years.

The effects have been severe. The drought has dried reservoirs, fueled wildfires, ruined crops, and put a heavy burden on the state's electric grid. In early September 2011, arid conditions sparked a series of wildfires across the state. The most devastating was the Bastrop Complex Fire in Bastrop County, which destroyed more than 1,300 homes and scorched over 34,000 acres.

Groundwater resources are threatened. In late January of 2012, wells in the town of Spicewood Beach officially ran out of water. Over a thousand households now depend on tanker trucks to deliver water to the town's storage tank. The Lower Colorado River Authority (LCRA), which owns the water system and is overseeing the emergency water operation, is trucking water into the town until a surface water treatment plant can supply water from Lake Travis.

In June 2013, Central Texas' Highland Lakes, the primary water reservoirs in the region, stood at thirty-nine percent capacity. The diminished water levels in Central Texas have devastated rice farmers near the coast who depend on water from those lakes. In March 2014, the combined lake levels remained below 850,000 acre-feet. This spurred the LCRA to sharply reduce water supplies to farmers in Matagorda, Wharton, and Colorado counties for the second year in a row.

The Texas AgriLife Extension Service estimates that the drought has cost farmers and ranchers nearly eight billion dollars. Corn outputs fell by forty percent in 2011 and peanut production has fallen as well. The price of hay has increased by two hundred percent, triggering a sharp increase in the price of feeding cattle. Ranchers have culled their herds, slaughtering or selling off large numbers of cattle in auctions to out-of-state buyers. After losing about 660,000 cattle during the drought, the state has its smallest herd since the 1950s. Rebuilding the state's cattle herd will not be cheap or easy because it can take years for pastures and grazing lands destroyed by drought to come back, and new animals must be bought or bred.

Texas is the nation's number three producer of agricultural products behind California and Iowa, so when crops and cattle fail there, prices can be expected to rise nationally.

Rains in June 2013 improved the outlook somewhat for agriculture, but the drought remained severe in much of the Texas Panhandle, an important agricultural region. The lack of crops has created conditions for severe dust storms across the western part of the state.

Water availability affects energy production. Nuclear, coal, and natural gas energy producers all require large amounts of fresh water to cool equipment. High demand for energy and scorching temperatures caused the Electric Reliability Council of Texas (ERCOT) to close one plant overnight during the height of the summer's heat.

According to the Texas Water Development Board, without additional water supplies Texas will be short 8.3 million acre-feet of water by 2060. It is a huge amount: a mere 3.07 acre-feet equals one million gallons. The board also estimates that failure to meet water needs in times of drought in 2060 could cost Texas businesses and workers up to $116 billion.

Climate Volatility and Food Production

While there are very heated discussions on the impact of human activity on climate trends and changes, just about everyone agrees that in recent decades global weather patterns have become increasingly volatile. The annual number of droughts, hurricanes, tsunamis, and floods has increased. As millions more move toward coastlines, the risk for human morbidity and mortality increases.

While the authors always consider scientific studies and predictions with an understanding that most sciences are imperfect and at the very least questionable in their statistical accuracy, the facts we have at hand for the past century suggest far beyond a reasonable doubt that the volatility of climate trends and cycles and their potentially negative effects are cause for concern.

These trends are having a profound effect on global agriculture. According to a study published in the journal *Science*, by the end of this century half of the world's population could face significant food shortages as rising temperatures shorten the growing season in the tropics and subtropics, where crops are less able to adjust to climate changes and food shortages are already starting to occur due to rapid population growth. Across huge areas of Central and South America, Africa, the Indian subcontinent, and Southeast Asia, climate change is likely to both increase the risk of drought and reduce the harvests of dietary staples such as rice and maize.

Scientists at the University of Washington and Stanford University, who collaborated on the study, postulate that by the year 2100 there is a ninety percent chance that the *coolest* temperatures in the tropics during the growing season will be higher than the *hottest* temperatures recorded in those regions through 2006. More temperate regions of the world can expect to see record-high temperatures and increased storm activity.

With the world population expected to double by the end of the century, humanity's limited food supply will become increasingly stretched. Rising temperatures will compel farmers to adjust their approach to agriculture, create new climate-appropriate crops, and develop advanced strategies to ensure adequate food supplies.

"When all the signs point in the same direction, and in this case it's a bad direction, you pretty much know what's going to happen," said David Battisti, a scientist at the University of Washington who led the study. "You're talking about hundreds of millions of additional people looking for food because they won't be able to find it where they find it now."

The tremendous push for the recognition global warming theory has not gone unchallenged. In fact some experts who have shown the consistent error in the math models would suggest that the fuzzy math used by others hides what may be a more disconcerting issue, global cooling. Bill Kirk, Cofounder and CEO of Weather Trends International, Inc. is a leading provider of weather predicting services for corporations and others that depend on his highly accurate predictions to make critical business decisions. Mr. Kirk points out that the last warming cycle lasted from 1976 to 2006 wherein a new cooling cycle began. The cooling cycle that ended in the mid-70s brought on warning of global cooling that were put to rest when the trend turned in the other direction shortly thereafter.

According to Kirk there are three major weather trends that will likely bring in a long cold cycle, perhaps one as severe as that seen since the seventeenth century. These three major cycles have not converged in this manner or timing for 400 years:

1. The **PDO or Pacific Decadal Oscillation Cycle** is a 30 year oceanic cycle of warm Pacific Ocean temps that ended in 2006 and turned cold in 2007.

2. The **AMO or Atlantic Multi-Decadal Oscillation Cycle** is a 20 year oceanic cycle of warm/cold Atlantic Ocean waters. This cycle, according to Kirk, should go cold within the next 5 years.

3. **11-Year Solar Cycles**. The sun is already in a 100 year weak cycle and current cycle 24 just came out of the maximum which was very weak. Many solar physicists say we're on the cusp of a 300-400 year solar minimum similar to that of the little ice age in the 1600s-1700s. This extremely weak cycle of the sun called the Maunder Minimum which occurred in the middle 1600s to early 1700s.

When all three team up there is strong evidence that we will have a very cold planet. We are already seeing the beginning of the trend with the cold Pacific Ocean. This alignment happened in part in the 1970s but with the exception of the sun in a phase of increasing output. Still, the 1970s were some of the snowiest in the past 100 years. Should the trends continue and all three of the phases converge the period from 2020 to 2040 could be exceptionally cold.

The important thing to remember is that because of the vast number of variables, we don't know the exact scope of the challenges we're going to face. It's likely that effective solutions will be unorthodox, unpredictable, and may come from "left field." The free market system, with its quickness of response and support of ingenuity, is best poised to produce the innovative solutions that we may so desperately need.

Homelessness in Haiti

The earthquake that devastated Haiti on January 12, 2010, directly affected an estimated three million people. Death toll estimates range as high as three hundred thousand. The government of Haiti has estimated that a quarter of a million homes and thirty thousand commercial buildings were either destroyed or severely damaged.

We cannot prevent earthquakes. But we can do much more to prepare for them and provide relief to those affected.

As of this writing, the results achieved in Haiti have been unsatisfactory. Homelessness remains a serious problem, and most sources estimate that three years after the Haitian earthquake, four hundred thousand people are still homeless. The *New York Times* has reported that these unfortunate people are spread among nearly five hundred camps, and that as of December 2012, only $215 million in international aid for the purpose of safe, affordable housing has been disbursed.

Life in the refugee camps is miserable. The homeless live in tents with tarps to keep out the rain. Residents are forced to survive as best they can without electricity or running water—often within sight of luxury hotels. Endless days of grinding poverty and idleness add to the despair.

According to a report by the International Organization for Migration, of the more than one million people left homeless by the 2010 earthquake, more than a third—just over 360,000—were still living in tents three years later.

The Haitian government seems to be misguided at best. Having failed at forcibly evicting people from some camps, the government is now trying to pay people to leave, to the amount of about four hundred and seventy US dollars. It claims that these "return cash grants" will cover a year of rent, but where? In August 2012, the *Times* reported that of the more than a quarter of a million houses damaged or destroyed by the earthquake, only fifteen thousand had been repaired and fewer than six thousand had been replaced. That leaves more than two hundred thousand families and former occupants with nowhere to go.

To the government, these are mere details. Hundreds of Haitian families have been forcibly evicted from refugee camps by Haiti's Civil Protection Agency. Many families were unable to gather their belongings before their homes were bulldozed. Reports say that in one of the evictions in a refugee camp outside of the capital Port-Au-Prince, evictions were carried out by a group of men armed with machetes and hammers.

No one seems to be able to manage the crisis, and people are taking the law into their own hands. In April 2013, Haitian attorney Reynold Georges decided that the thirty thousand people who were living on his property had to go. He arrived with a judge and a police officer at what's called Camp Acra, a vast jumble of tents and plywood shacks dotting a rocky hillside in the heart of the Haitian capital. The lawyer told the people that they were squatting on his land and had to leave. If they didn't vacate, he said he'd have the shelters burned down and leveled by bulldozers. Some residents responded by lobbing rocks at Georges and his associates.

The encounter set off a series of events that left several shelters burned and a camp resident dead. It occurred about a week before the human rights group Amnesty International issued a report on the dramatic increase in camp evictions in Haiti during the past year.

It's not just houses that aren't getting built. Despite a 2010 promise by then-French Foreign Minister Bernard Kouchner and others to spend seventy million dollars to rebuild the General Hospital in Port-au-Prince, as of this writing—three years later—the work has not begun. The *New York Times* reported in December 2012 that preparation of patients for surgery was being done in a section of the building that was missing its outside walls. It could be said that the results of even the greatest intentions of governments often reflect the convolution of the systems from which they must pass.

Burning Wood for Fuel in Africa

Because of the nearly ubiquitous availability of electricity and natural gas, it may be difficult for Americans to understand that in many parts of the world wood is still the fuel of choice.

The 2007 United Nations Food and Agriculture Organization Forest Report revealed that in Africa, almost ninety percent of all wood removals are used for energy. In most developing regions, deforestation and forest degradation continue to be a serious problem. A reversal of the situation would require structural changes in economies to reduce direct and indirect dependence on land. However, in most developing tropical countries the use of agricultural land for both subsistence and commercial cultivation continues to expand. Consequently, the rate of deforestation is expected to continue.

In 2000, nearly 470 million tons of wood were consumed in Sub-Saharan African homes in the form of firewood and charcoal. Per capita, this is more than is used in any other region in the world. China and India together burned nearly one-third less wood in the same year, despite a combined population that is more than three times that of Sub-Saharan Africa. While heating and cooking will remain the principal uses for fuel-wood and charcoal in developing countries, the use of solid biofuels for the production of electricity is expected to triple by 2030.

For many developing countries, wood will remain the most important source of energy. The rising price of oil and increasing concern for climate change will result in increased use of wood as fuel in both developed and developing countries. In some government circles the burning of wood is seen as non-objectionable because wood is considered a "renewable biomass." The assumption is that burned wood can be re-grown, and that the new growth will absorb as much CO_2 from the atmosphere as was released in the burning of it. The fact that burning wood releases more greenhouse gases per unit of energy released than burning oil or natural gas does is conveniently overlooked.

Some of the drawbacks of the use of fuel-wood, such as deforestation, may seem obvious. But there are other hidden dangers. Unless deeply ingrained habits of fuel use are changed, it is estimated that by 2030, eight million children and two million women will die prematurely of pulmonary disease.

This is a serious problem for which, as we will see in a subsequent chapter, a promising solution has been developed by free market entrepreneurs.

The 2004 Indian Ocean Earthquake and Tsunami

The Indian Ocean earthquake was a huge undersea event that occurred on Sunday, December 26, 2004. With an epicenter off the west coast of Sumatra, Indonesia, the quake triggered a series of devastating tsunamis along the coasts of the Indian Ocean, killing over 230,000 people in fourteen countries. Indonesia was the hardest hit country, followed by Sri

Lanka, India, and Thailand. Hundreds of thousands of homes and businesses were destroyed, instantly creating a vast population of homeless tsunami refugees.

It was one of the deadliest natural disasters in recorded history.

The global humanitarian response was massive. The primary concern of relief and government agencies was to provide sanitation facilities and fresh drinking water to contain the spread of diseases such as cholera, diphtheria, dysentery, typhoid and hepatitis A and B. Long-term challenges included rebuilding thousands of destroyed homes and buildings, resettling families, repairs to public infrastructure, and regenerating local economies. All of this took money, and nations all over the world pledged over fourteen billion dollars in aid for damaged regions.

A little more than a week after the disaster, on January 5, Jan Egeland commented that too many countries were making pledges without any guarantee that the funds would arrive. In mid-March 2005, the Asian Development Bank reported that the provision of over four billion dollars in aid promised by governments was behind schedule. As the BBC reported, Sri Lanka's Foreign Minister Lakshman Kadirgamar criticized the nations and organizations that had loudly pledged donations. "Not a penny has come through yet," he said. "We are doing the relief work with our government money. Sri Lanka is still waiting for the money pledged by the donors. Money pledged by the people has been pledged to the NGOs. A lot of aid which has been coming in latterly is, I'm afraid I'm sorry to say, not very useful. For instance, there was a container full of teddy bears. They're obviously given with good will; nobody says 'no' to that...For instance we do not need rice. We are expecting a bumper harvest, anyone who sends rice is wasting their time and money."

In February 2006, a year after the tsunami, AsiaNews reported that survivors of the disaster in Tamil Nadu and Andaman in India had received "more words than concrete action" from the government. They were in urgent need of a comprehensive rehabilitation program, but felt as though they were forgotten by the international community and their own government. The reasons behind the lack of relief were "corruption and the need to finance future election campaigns with money destined for tsunami relief."

Two years after the disaster, on December 26, 2006, Seth Mydans of the *New York Times* reported that by some estimates only one-third of the aid pledged to victims had been distributed to affected countries. To make matters worse, much of that had been lost to mismanagement, corruption, political infighting, and bureaucratic red tape. Hundreds of thousands of people were still without permanent homes or jobs, and the very real possibility existed that many victims were fated to live out the rest of their lives as refugees of the tsunami. In Sri Lanka, the revival of a civil war made life even more precarious for survivors. In India, the British aid group Oxfam estimated that two years after the crisis, seventy percent of affected people still lived in temporary shelters.

The answer to the long-term success of these people is found in their ability to establish a dependable livelihood free of dependence on donations and outside assistance. That independence builds communities when there is security in their work and confidence in the likelihood that they will be able to provide for the long run.

Cyclone Nargis

Over the centuries, Myanmar, formerly known as Burma, has suffered its share of violent storms. But nothing in modern history can compare with Cyclone Nargis. Gaining immense power over the Bay of Bengal, the first named storm of the 2008 North Indian Ocean cyclone season developed in late April and quickly strengthened to attain peak wind speeds of over one hundred and thirty miles an hour. On May 2, 2008, the cyclone moved ashore in the Ayeyarwady Division of Myanmar at maximum intensity and, after passing near the major city of Yangon (formerly Rangoon), gradually weakened until dissipating two days later near the border of Myanmar and Thailand.

The massive cyclone sent a storm surge thirty miles up the densely populated Irrawaddy delta, causing devastating destruction and at least 146,000 fatalities. The Labutta Township, which is about twenty-five miles inland, was reported to have eighty thousand dead, with about ten thousand more deaths in Bogale, another town on the broad Irrawaddy delta located about twenty miles east of Labutta. Foreign aid workers working in Myanmar estimated that two to three million people were left homeless.

Damage was estimated at over ten billion dollars, which made it the most destructive cyclone ever recorded in this basin. It blew away seven hundred thousand homes in the delta. In the town of Labutta, state television reported that seventy-five percent of buildings had collapsed and that one building in five had their roofs ripped off. Another report suggested that ninety-five percent of buildings in the Irrawaddy delta area were destroyed. Burst sewage mains caused the landscape to flood with waste, ruining the rice crop. Survivors faced horrific conditions in basic subsistence; markets were closed and local food prices doubled or tripled. It killed three-fourths of the livestock, sank half the fishing fleet, and salted a million acres of rice paddies with its seawater surges. Many rice farmers lost their seeds and were unprepared to plant their crop, which they normally did during the month of May to be harvested in November.

The Myanmar government's official death toll was certainly underreported, and there have been allegations that government officials halted the death count after 138,000 to minimize political backlash. The actual death toll from Nargis is estimated to be 146,000, including ninety thousand people confirmed dead and fifty-six thousand missing. Since most of the missing were never located, it has been assumed that these people were killed. It is now believed that hundreds of thousands of victims will never be found because their bodies have decayed, were buried, or were washed out to sea.

The atrocious behavior of Myanmar's ruling military junta before, during, and after the crisis has been well documented, and its consequences will be explored in depth in the following chapter of this book. According to reports, forty-eight hours before the cyclone hit the country's coast, authorities in India had warned the Myanmar government about the danger that Cyclone Nargis posed. Little preparation was made. After the cyclone had passed, relief efforts were slowed as Myanmar's rulers initially resisted large-scale international aid. The junta finally accepted aid a few days after India's request was accepted. Some donated aid items were later found to be available in the country's black market.

To compound the crisis, only ten days after the Cyclone Nargis devastated Myanmar, nearby central China was hit by the massive Sichuan earthquake, the costliest disaster in Chinese history and the third costliest disaster ever known.

The Great Sichuan Earthquake

On Monday afternoon, May 12, 2008, a violent earthquake rocked Sichuan Province in southwestern China. Tremors were felt in nearby countries and as far away as both Beijing and Shanghai, where office buildings swayed. For months after the main quake, strong aftershocks continued to hit the area, causing new casualties and damage. The twenty-first deadliest earthquake of all time, it was the deadliest earthquake to hit China since the 1976

Tangshan earthquake, which killed at least 240,000 people, and was the strongest in the country since the 1950 Chayu earthquake, which registered at 8.5 on the Richter magnitude scale.

The Great Sichuan Earthquake killed 69,195 people, with 18,392 reported missing. It left about 4.8 million people homeless, though some sources put the number as high as eleven million. Approximately fifteen million people lived in the affected areas.

Both the Shanghai Stock Exchange and the Shenzhen Stock Exchange suspended trading of companies based in southwestern China. Copper rose over speculations that production in southwestern China might have been affected, and oil prices dropped over speculations that demand from China would fall.

Immediately after the earthquake event, all Internet capabilities were cut to the Sichuan area, and mobile and terrestrial telecommunications were cut to other affected areas. China Mobile had more than twenty-three hundred base stations suspended due to power disruption or severe telecommunication traffic congestion. Half of the wireless communications were lost in the Sichuan province. China Unicom's service in Wenchuan and four nearby counties was cut off, with more than seven hundred towers suspended.

Over the next several months, as the situation in the Sichuan province gradually improved, elements of telecommunications were restored by the government. Eventually, a handful of major news and media websites were made accessible online in the region.

One of the most appalling aspects of the earthquake was the uncovering of a pattern of shoddy and unsafe school construction throughout the region. At least seven thousand school buildings throughout the province collapsed, killing thousands of children. In Mianyang City, seven schools collapsed, burying at least 1,700 people. At least six hundred students and staff died at Juyuan Elementary School, and up to 1,300 children and teachers died at Beichuan Middle School. In the city of Dujiangyan, southeast of the epicenter, an entire school collapsed, leaving nine hundred students buried. Fewer than sixty survived. The Juyuan Middle School, where many teenagers were buried, was excavated by civilians and cranes. Another seven hundred students were buried in a school in Hanwang.

In China, even after a horrific disaster and the deaths of thousands of children, it was business as usual. It's no secret that China suffers from widespread and deeply rooted corruption—graft, bribery, embezzlement, backdoor deals, nepotism, patronage, and statistical falsification. Corruption destroys the legitimacy of the Chinese Communist Party (CCP), undermines the environment, exacerbates economic inequality, and fuels social unrest. Greater economic freedom has not slowed down corruption, but instead it's grown even more entrenched and cancerous in its character and scope. Business deals are often not possible without corruption. Experts agree that failure to contain widespread corruption is among the most serious threats to China's future economic and political stability.

In Transparency International's "Corruption Perceptions Index" for 2012, China was ranked eightieth out of one hundred and seventy-six countries. This puts the world's second largest economy in the company of Serbia, El Salvador, Jamaica, Burkina Faso, and Morocco.

The Somalia Famine

Over the course of centuries, civilizations rise and fall. They flourish and then, whether by natural forces or human conflict, they wither. Nowhere is this more evident than in Somalia. Ancient pyramidal structures, tombs, stone walls, and ruined cities found in this desert nation are a testament to the ancient and sophisticated civilizations that once thrived on the Horn of Africa. The findings of archaeological excavations and research in the area reveal that over three thousand years ago this civilization was an important center for commercial activity with the rest of the ancient world, had an ancient writing system, and enjoyed a lucrative trading relationship with Ancient Egypt and Mycenaean Greece.

Today, those former glories are distant memories. With a population of about ten million, Somalia has a per capita gross domestic product (GDP) of six hundred dollars. (In contrast, the per capita GDP of Egypt is $6,650, and in the United States it's $49,900.)

Somalia has not had a central government since 1991 when the Siad Barre regime was overthrown. The violent civil war disrupted agriculture and food distribution in southern Somalia. The causes of the conflict were clan allegiances and competition for resources between the warring clans. Various factions competed for influence in the power vacuum that followed, which in the mid-1990s precipitated an aborted UN peacekeeping mission. Throughout the 1990s most of southern Somalia was under the authority of local warlords or militias. Fighting among these militias was one of the causes of the devastating 1992–93 famine, which affected roughly the same area as the 2011 famine.

Nearly 260,000 people died during the famine that ravaged Somalia from 2010 to 2012. (It's called the 2011 famine because that's when famine was officially declared, but it started the year before.) Half of the victims were children under the age of five. In southern and central Somalia, an estimated 4.6% of the total population died, including ten percent of children under five. In Lower Shebelle, eighteen percent of children under five died, and in Mogadishu the number was seventeen percent.

The crisis was caused by both natural and human forces—primarily a severe drought combined with conflict between rival groups fighting for power. During the extreme drought in 2011 that affected more than thirteen million people across the Horn of Africa, Somalia was worst hit. The drought and the civil unrest forced tens of thousands of people to flee their homes in search of food. Another cause of the crisis included the rapidly rising price of food, both domestically in Somalia and globally. Even in years with good rainfall, Somalia relies heavily on imported food—both commercial imports and, for many years, food aid. Any increase in the international price of food worsens the perpetual food access crisis in Somalia.

The UN said that to lessen the scope of the disaster, humanitarian aid needed to have been provided much more quickly. Rudi Van Aaken, the deputy head of the FAO mission in Somalia, told the BBC that the response had been too slow. "I think the main lesson learned is that the humanitarian community should be ready to take early action—respond early on. Responding only when the famine is declared is very, very ineffective. Actually, about half of the casualties were there before the famine was already declared."

The UN first declared a famine in July 2011 in Somalia's Southern Bakool and Lower Shebelle regions. These areas were controlled not by the government but by the militant Islamist group al-Shabab, which is aligned to al-Qaeda. Al-Shabab denied there was a famine and prohibited Western aid agencies from operating within territory under its control. The famine later spread to Middle Shebelle, Afgoye, and to the camps for displaced people in the government-controlled capital, Mogadishu. Ravaged by nearly uninterrupted civil war for the previous two decades, Somalia was one of the most dangerous places in the world for aid workers but one of the regions that needed them most.

The UN declared the famine over in February 2012. "While conditions in Somalia have improved in recent months, the country still has one of the highest rates of child malnutrition and infant mortality in the world," Ben Foot, from the charity Save the Children, said in a statement.

Recovery has been slow and incomplete. Today, more than a million Somalis are refugees in surrounding nations, and another million are displaced inside the country.

.

Chapter Two: Government Solutions Fall Short

Every human being desires and deserves a modicum of stability in their lives. We all need a steady supply of food and clean water. We all need household and community energy that will be there for us day after day. We all need sturdy housing that provides shelter and withstands the elements.

These things require constancy. Our water must flow reliably and our crops must grow every season. Our energy sources—the sun, hydrocarbons, wind—must be dependable and consistent. Our houses and buildings need to have permanence and strength.

While it is perfectly understandable that we strive for stability, the world does not conduct its affairs with our benefit in mind. Change is the law of nature, not stasis. Change happens both very slowly and very quickly. Can governments be expected to provide completely for the long-term stability of all citizens without outside assistance? The evidence overwhelmingly suggests the answer is No.

For example, consider earthquakes. The planet we inhabit is not a solid rock; it is constantly changing. The very thin outer crust of the earth—the lithosphere—is not one continuous surface like an eggshell. It's more like a soccer ball, with sections stitched together. These sections are called tectonic plates. The surface of the earth is made up of roughly eight large tectonic plates and a dozen smaller ones. They are not stationary; over time, they move and jostle one another. Where they rub against each other there is friction, and this causes earthquakes. The North American tectonic plate—the immense slab of the earth's crust that supports the United States, Canada, Greenland, and part of Siberia and Japan—is moving in a southwesterly direction at a rate of about two centimeters per year. The movement is very slow but it never stops. In contrast, the motion that is produced by plates rubbing against each other can be fast and violent. Earthquakes are most likely to happen along the borders of the plates where they jostle each other.

The Northridge earthquake occurred just before dawn on January 17, 1994, in Reseda, a neighborhood in Los Angeles, California. It lasted for about twenty seconds. The 6.7 magnitude earthquake was felt as far away as Las Vegas, Nevada, about 220 miles from the epicenter. When it was over, the death toll came to a total of fifty-seven people and there were nearly nine thousand injured. The Northridge earthquake caused an estimated twenty billion dollars in damage, making it one of the costliest natural disasters in U.S. history.

In terms of events that happen on the planet earth, which is a massive object, it was like a mosquito landing on an elephant. Yet for humans living in the area it was hugely destructive.

Violent change can be quickly destructive. All change, both slow and rapid, creates uncertainty and risk.

Change is constant, and therefore we cannot eliminate risk from our lives.

Many of our challenges are caused by natural forces. They are the manifestation of the fact that we inhabit an unsteady planet spinning through a hazardous universe. Earthquakes violently destroy buildings and roads. Volcanoes spew toxic dust high into the atmosphere. The awesome energy of the sun heats the earth and creates swirling currents of air and water. Living on the earth's surface, we are pummeled by hurricanes and typhoons. Droughts turn fertile farmland into bowls of dust. All of these events, and countless more of every variety, injure us, kill us, and contribute to early death.

Many more challenges are of our own making. In our continuing drive to learn how to manage ourselves and our planet, we make terrible mistakes. Government policies that are designed to promote stability and improve our lives often have the opposite effect. Food supplies are squandered. Water is mismanaged. Urban planning creates not progress but blight and slums. Energy policies create waste and stifle innovation. Not only are mistakes made, but humans too often act out of greed or even with evil intent. Expensive wars are waged, we steal from each other, and we create laws that promote one group at the expense of another. As governments grow in respective size and power, there is a natural tendency toward inefficiency. The goals of governments are often colored by a need to validate and promote the government itself, with lessened consideration for the often more efficient solutions produced through the ingenuity of the people in an entrepreneurial society.

How then can we manage change and achieve real sustainable progress? How can we leverage the size and potential efficiencies of government with the innovations and solutions that are championed by free market models? Public-private partnerships are a start, but we believe the goal is integrated systems that utilize the best of both worlds.

We know that we cannot eliminate risk from the human experience. As long as we inhabit a planet whose tectonic plates are shifting under our feet, as long as the sun's energy creates violent weather patterns, as long as pathogens exist, we will not be free of risk. Change, not stasis, is the law of the universe. The conditions that exist today will be different tomorrow. It will rain where there once was desert. A source of fuel will dry up and another one will emerge. We will make new discoveries in science and medicine. There will be breakthroughs in technology. And above all, we humans will always be subject to natural disasters and to the cruel calculus of accidents and disease.

We cannot alter the fact that the universe is always changing and is full of risk. What we can do, and what we have done with limited success over the course of many centuries, is reduce risk from natural disasters. We can anticipate events such as floods and hurricanes. We can construct buildings to withstand earthquakes. We can cure many previously fatal diseases. We can manage water resources to provide sustainable supplies. We can grow enough food to provide for every human on the planet.

While humans have had modest success in discovering and preparing for the endless calamities of nature that regularly afflict us, there are still millions who die every year, not for a lack of technology or resources, but for lack of efficient relief systems. The grand inefficiency in many government-focused approaches stems from the tendency by both public and private participants to regularly consider the burden for certain categories of solutions as solely falling upon government.

As we reflect upon the totality of human experience, and particularly upon the brief survey of tragedies presented in the first chapter of this book, we ask ourselves what organizations or institutions have the best track records of providing innovative solutions. What works to relieve suffering and advance the human condition? And, in contrast, what doesn't work as well?

Experience has shown us some basic truths. Over the centuries, and persisting to this day, we can see that on a long-term global basis the most damaging and yet preventable causes of human misery are often government policies that attempt to force stasis upon a world in which change is the natural law. When a government, in attempting to solve a problem or reduce risk for its citizens, enacts legislation to establish policy or restrict behavior, it is attempting to both correct some perceived problem in the past and to ensure that the problem does not recur in the future. This works very well, for example, with human rights legislation that affirms the basic dignity and freedom of every human being. But this same rigid legislative approach does not work so well—and in fact can lead to disaster—when it attempts to impose an artificial plan on events that will take place in the future. In recent history we have seen time and time again where governments, whether acting out of a sense of benevolence or from some darker motivation, have impeded progress by seeking to impose an inflexible plan on future events or—even worse—by enacting legislation that is simply wrongheaded and damaging. Such attempts may temporarily please one group or another, but the relentless rate of change often destroys whatever benefit the plan had at its inception.

In recent history, the worst and most obvious examples of horrific government planning have been the attempts by the one-party socialist state of the former Soviet Union to plan and control every aspect of both industrial and agricultural production. In the vast Soviet bureaucracy, unqualified party hacks, chosen not for their competence but for their loyalty to the party and the dictator, attempted to create rigid plans and production quotas for every conceivable consumer item from bread to automobiles. Workers were assigned to whatever job the party chose. Factories were built and operated by party loyalists who had no other motivation other than pleasing the party bosses and avoiding the secret police. The result of this orgy of government control was the deaths of millions of citizens—often by starvation—and the continued mediocrity of every aspect of everyday life in every town and village of the Soviet Union.

The former Soviet Union may be the most obvious example of the failure of government planning in the modern era, but if you look around the globe you see it echoes everywhere.

In this book we'll not overlook the truly depraved dictatorships that bring their nations to ruin, but as we shine the spotlight on them we freely recognize that such governments are easy targets. Their crimes are obvious and it's clear to any rational human being that an oppressive dictatorship is bad news for any people or nation.

We'll also not overlook the destructive potential of political conflict within democracies, which too often produce government policies that either favor one special interest group over another or, even more often, produce mediocre results that satisfy no one.

Such political conflict has been with mankind for centuries and will almost certainly be with us for centuries to come. And while the free market system is clearly preferable to a political system that is fraught with paralyzing conflict, the immediate solution must first be the easing of the political climate. A good example of this is the tenure of Margaret Thatcher as prime minister of the United Kingdom from 1979 to 1990; her clearheaded policies triumphed over the previous decade of petty political bickering and helped put the UK back on the road to being a global economic force.

While acknowledging the damage caused by both outright dictatorships and by central governments that are diseased by political paralysis and bloat, we hope to focus sharply on that huge grey area of what we will call benevolent bungling. Because of political forces, self-interest, ignorance, laziness, or a misplaced desire to eliminate all risk, governments often start out with good intentions and wind up by not solving the problem. After a disaster, people are not fed, shelter is not provided, energy systems fail, and water is contaminated, not because people in government don't mean well, but because the system just can't work the way we want it to. Good intentions cannot be transformed into good results. It's no one's fault; people do what they can do.

It's like asking an elephant to thread a needle. The elephant may be friendly and may be tame, and may even possess exceptional intelligence. But threading a needle requires nimbleness and a high degree of precision. No matter how hard or how long he tries, the elephant will not get the thread through the needle.

It's just not the job for him.

The Kaalokol Fish Processing Plant

Within the great Kenyan Rift Valley in Africa lies Lake Turkana. With its far northern end crossing into Ethiopia, it is both the world's largest permanent desert lake and the world's largest alkaline lake. The lake is home to about fifty species of fish, which, in terms of global lake biology, is a relatively low number. In contrast, before overfishing, Lake Victoria was home to over five hundred species.

The Turkana are people native to the Turkana District in northwest Kenya, a semi-arid climate region that borders Lake Turkana in the east. According to the 2009 Kenyan census,

Turkana number 855,399, or 2.5% of the Kenyan population. Turkana is a very poor remote province, very underdeveloped, and vulnerable to the whims of drought.

The Turkana are noted for raising camels and weaving baskets. They are a herding and hunting people; goats, camels, donkeys and zebu are their primary herd stock. In this society, livestock functions not only as a source of milk and meat but as currency used for bride-price negotiations and dowries.

The men often go hunting to catch dik-dik, wildebeest, wild pig, antelope, marsh deer, hare, and other game animals. The Turkana are not interested in fishing. Indeed, in some parts of Turkana society fishing is expressly taboo. Wealth is measured in livestock, and only those who are destitute and starving would consider catching and eating fish.

Meanwhile, 4,426 miles to the north of Turkana—about nine hours by air to Oslo—is the headquarters of the Norwegian Agency for Development Cooperation (NORAD), *not to be confused with the North American Aerospace Defense Command, which is also abbreviated NORAD*. It's a directorate under the Norwegian Ministry of Foreign Affairs. Its task is to ensure effective foreign aid, with quality assurance and evaluation.

What do the Turkana and the Norwegian Agency for Development Cooperation have in common?

The Lake Turkana fish processing plant.

In the early 1980s the Norwegian development agency decided that exploiting the resources of Lake Turkana would be a good economic initiative for the region. Such an effort would increase incomes, boost employment, and bring stability. Despite the fact that the Turkana are nomads with no history of fishing or eating fish, the Norwegian government saw a perfect opportunity in the vast but underutilized lake that seemed to be teeming with uncaught fish. With these intentions, the Kaalokol fish factory was designed and built, and the agency set about teaching Turkana's largely herding communities how to harvest the lake's fish stocks to bring income into the poverty-stricken region. "Norway felt this is a district that has been neglected by the state," Pippi Soegaard, first secretary of the Norwegian development agency in Kenya, told Reuters on a trip to Turkana.

The Turkana herders were trained and hired as fishers and factory workers.

The plant was completed and operated for a few days, but then was quickly shut down. The problem was that the longstanding traditions and nomadic culture of the population had been overlooked by the decision-makers at the top, and the project had been implemented without first consulting with the community. The factory proved to be an unsustainable business due to its geographical remoteness, the nomadic culture of the workers needed to keep it up and running, and the cultural perspective on fishing in general in a society where owning cattle is a sign of wealth. The cost to operate the freezers and the demand for clean water in the desert were too high.

Turkana's remoteness, cut off from the rest of Kenya by poor roads, few telephones, and little electricity, makes it a difficult place to sustain a fishing business. The factory was running on generators, and the costs were more than could be earned back. Fish is a product that perishes fast, and the plant's location was far from the end consumer. Maintaining a cold chain—where food is frozen at the source and then transported to market—in an undeveloped country is expensive.

Since the Turkana are not fishermen, another challenge was bringing in outsiders with fishing expertise. Inviting experienced fishermen from other regions to start businesses could ignite conflict in an already volatile region, where nomadic tribes have a history of friction.

The project was doomed from its initial conception because it was not based on the demands and leadership of the community. What a Norwegian development organization considers a viable career and way of life cannot be simply transplanted into a new environment and be expected to be embraced.

Analysts also cite a diplomatic conflict between Norway and ex-president Daniel arap Moi, who briefly broke off diplomatic ties with Norway in 1990 after accusing it of sheltering dissident politicians. "Moi didn't realize that if you throw out an ambassador the aid would also go," Soegaard said. "(The factory) ended as an unsuccessful program in the middle of nowhere." Ties were restored in 1994 but development aid resumed only in 2004. Soegaard did not know how much money was pumped into the factory itself, but estimated that Norway spent about one billion Norwegian crowns ($152 million) in today's money in Turkana over twenty years, on the factory and on regional community projects.

"It was the old top-bottom approach," said Cheanati Wasike, government fisheries officer for Lake Turkana. "The lake was identified by outsiders as a resource but they never consulted the Turkana, never asked them what they thought of fishing it."

Despite occasional talk about its revival, the Kaalokol fish processing plant remains a rusting hulk in Kenya's arid northwest. It's a classic example of good intentions and government planning that run smack into the solid wall of reality.

Should this effort have been made by a group of private investors, the likelihood is that the research would have been more thorough as the investment would require a higher level of accountability than what is typical of a government funded project. At the very least, the failed efforts would have been born by a group willing to take a measured risk for an opportunity at a profitable business, but instead the tax payers are strapped with the cost of failure.

The Fukushima Daiichi Nuclear Power Plant Disaster

It was the most powerful known tremor ever to have hit Japan and the fifth most powerful earthquake in the world since modern record-keeping began in 1900. The 2011 earthquake off the Pacific coast of Tōhoku, often referred to in Japan as the Great East Japan Earthquake, caused immense destruction not only from the earthquake itself but by the subsequent tsunami.

At 2:45 PM on Friday, March 11, 2011, at a spot approximately forty-three miles east of the Oshika Peninsula of Tōhoku and at an underwater depth of approximately nineteen miles, two of the earth's tectonic plates shifted. Honshu, the main island of Japan, slid eight feet to the east and dropped as much as two feet lower. On a global scale, the jostling of the tectonic plates moved the earth's mass closer to its center, causing the earth's rotation to speed up by 1.8 millionths of a second, and even changing the tilt of the earth's axis.

The undersea upheaval triggered a series of powerful tsunami waves. Just over an hour after the earthquake, a tsunami flooded Sendai Airport, which is located near the coast of Miyagi Prefecture, with multiple waves sweeping away cars and planes and flooding buildings as they traveled inland. Waves reached heights of up to 133 feet in Miyako, and in the Sendai area traveled up to six miles inland. A four-meter high tsunami hit Iwate Prefecture, and Wakabayashi Ward in Sendai was also hard hit.

The coastal devastation was massive and unprecedented.

The Japanese National Police Agency report issued in September 2011 confirmed 15,883 deaths, 6,145 injured, and 2,656 people missing across twenty prefectures, as well as

129,225 buildings totally collapsed, with a further 254,204 buildings "half collapsed", and another 691,766 buildings partially damaged. The earthquake and tsunami also caused extensive and severe structural damage in northeastern Japan, including heavy damage to roads and railways as well as fires in many areas, and a dam collapse. Around 4.4 million households in northeastern Japan were left without electricity and 1.5 million without water.

Save the Children reported that as many as 100,000 children were uprooted from their homes, some of whom were separated from their families because the earthquake occurred during the school day.

Early estimates placed insured losses from the earthquake alone to be as high as $34.6 billion. The World Bank's estimated economic cost was $235 billion, making it the costliest natural disaster in world history.

Japanese Prime Minister Naoto Kan said, "In the sixty-five years after the end of World War II, this is the toughest and the most difficult crisis for Japan."

If the earthquake and tsunami weren't bad enough, there soon unfolded the disaster at the Fukushima Daiichi nuclear power plant, operated by the Tokyo Electric Power Company, or TEPCO. It became the largest nuclear disaster since the Chernobyl meltdown of 1986 and only the second disaster (along with Chernobyl) to measure Level 7 on the International Nuclear Event Scale.

The tsunami flooded the plant's nuclear reactors. As the situation grew out of control at the plant, the Japanese government initially evacuated all residents within a twelve-mile radius of the complex before expanding the order to nineteen miles; an area that was home to roughly 150,000 residents. The United States advised its citizens to stay at least fifty miles away from the Fukushima plant. The US advisory was criticized by some, perhaps because within a fifty-mile radius of the plant there were living some two million people—a much larger refugee problem if they all had to leave.

As of this writing, more than two years after the earthquake, tsunami, and Fukushima disaster, the lives of tens of thousands of people have still not returned to normal. For them the disasters continue.

One investigation was made by the National Diet of Japan Fukushima Nuclear Accident Independent Investigation Commission (NAIIC), the commission formed by the statutory law enactment by the Diet of Japan on October 7, 2011.

On July 5, 2012, the NAIIC panel delivered a stern verdict in the form of a preliminary eighty-eight-page executive summary. Although such an event should have been predicted and planned for, the panel said it found huge gaps in safety standards and emergency procedures. Among other findings, the report said:

"The disaster was natural but the panic and confusion were manmade.

"The earthquake and tsunami of March 11, 2011 were natural disasters of a magnitude that shocked the entire world. Although triggered by these cataclysmic events, the subsequent accident at the Fukushima Daiichi Nuclear Power Plant cannot be regarded as a natural disaster. It was a profoundly manmade disaster—that could and should have been foreseen and prevented.

"Our report catalogues a multitude of errors and willful negligence that left the Fukushima plant unprepared for the events of March 11. And it examines serious deficiencies in the response to the accident by TEPCO, regulators and the government.

"For all the extensive detail it provides, what this report cannot fully convey—especially to a global audience—is the mindset that supported the negligence behind this disaster. What must be admitted—very painfully—is that this was a disaster 'Made in Japan.'"

Chapter Three: Free Market Solutions

What we have presented in the previous chapters is only a brief survey of the many calamities that afflict human existence here on earth. These disasters, which are costly both in terms of direct loss of human life and the degradation of the quality of life, have been happening for as long as we've inhabited this planet. We do not live in an environment that is stable and where sudden change is predictable. Destructive weather events, climate changes, and earthquakes are repeating phenomena that we know are going to happen; we just don't know exactly where and when.

For example, while some regions such as the Pacific Rim are known to have a high risk for earthquakes, surprises can happen anywhere.

At 1:51 PM on August 23, 2011, residents of New York City felt an unfamiliar sensation: the earth was shaking, and not from a subway train. For thirty seconds a powerful earthquake, centered in Virginia, sent tremors from Hampstead, North Carolina in the south, northward to the nation's capital, to New York City, and as far as Concord, New Hampshire. Because of the population density of the East Coast, the quake was reportedly felt by more people than any other quake in United States history.

Fortunately, no deaths and only minor injuries were reported. But the possibility for a real disaster was clear. The streets of downtown Washington, D.C. filled with thousands of people as buildings from the capital to the White House were evacuated. The Washington Metro system's trains were forced to operate at reduced speeds while tracks and tunnels were inspected. Cracks appeared near the top of the Washington Monument, the world's tallest stone structure, which was promptly closed for repairs and may not reopen until 2014. Buildings throughout major metropolitan centers in the northeast were evacuated after the quake. The quake temporarily shuttered New York airports and delayed flights along the East Coast, prompted crack inspections of the Holland Tunnel, snarled cell-phone service—and put to rest the idea that big quakes are the sole province of the West Coast.

Unpredictable? Yes. Impossible? Not at all. Guaranteed to happen again? Yes. But no one knows when it will happen or how catastrophic the event will be. Disasters can happen anywhere in the world at virtually any time.

We have seen how governments prepare for disasters and respond to them. (In the case of the 2011 Virginia quake, there was zero preparation.) Historically and globally, the record of response is not good. Governments, especially those in less developed countries, tend to be underprepared for calamity and slow to respond when calamity strikes. Why? Because of the inefficient nature of well-meaning democratic governments and the callous nature of corrupt dictatorships. The planning required for disaster response is too complex and riddled with competing special interests, and the costs of a quick response are often too high.

This is not to say that human beings are by nature not generous. After some disasters, such as the massive 2010 Haiti earthquake, relief money pours in from governments, organizations, and individuals who want to help. Indeed, science is now discovering that humans are naturally hard-wired to be generous. A recent article in the *Wall Street Journal* by Elizabeth Svoboda revealed that by using advanced tools like fMRI, scientists are identifying the circuits within the brain that govern philanthropic social impulses. A body of data is starting to fill the gap about the origins of the human desire to help others, and there is evidence of a biological imperative that spurs altruism.

The inherent generosity of humans is not the problem. The challenge facing victims of disasters is that donated money too often seems to vanish into thin air, or donations are made of stuff that makes the donor feel good about themselves but does not truly benefit the victims.

It doesn't matter what type of crisis we must respond to; the results are often not what we want or intend. Some disasters, such as power failures, are manmade. Others, such as floods, are often made worse by human ineptitude. We have seen how governments have all too often helped to create a disaster by poor regulation, corruption, inefficiency, or political shenanigans.

The seriousness of the problems is obvious, and it's equally clear that in too many cases the solutions that are offered by governments do not work. But the goal of this book is not to simply offer complaints or to point out fault in others. Such an attitude would not be helpful to either beleaguered governments or to victims.

We propose, and believe in, a radical rethinking of disaster relief that focuses not only on government responses but responses rooted in the free market system.

Why free markets? Because over the centuries, free markets have consistently been the source of innovation, wealth generation, and problem solving on a scale that has transformed human civilization.

The Nature of Free Markets

Before we go further, let's take a few minutes to discuss the concept of free markets and what this really means. Of course, it is not the intent of this book to offer a detailed discussion of free market economics; such an effort would fill volumes, and indeed you can go to any library and find endless shelves of scholarly tomes devoted to the subject. It's our much more modest goal to highlight the advantages of a free market approach to disaster relief.

At its most simplistic, a free market is where goods or services can be exchanged without limitation to the benefit of both parties. The key is that both parties benefit from the exchange. Both gain something that they need or want. For example, John is walking along with money in his pocket but he has no food. The grocer, on the other hand, has plenty of food but is anxious to acquire money. And so, finding each other, they strike a deal. John buys food from the grocer. Each one values their respective goods or services differently, and these differences set the scene for an exchange.

This simple scenario stands in stark contrast to the argument against free trade offered by the mercantilist period of sixteenth- to eighteenth-century Europe and expounded by the famed sixteenth-century French essayist Michel de Montaigne. The mercantilists argued that in any trade, one party can benefit only at the expense of the other, and that in every transaction there must be a winner and a loser, an "exploiter" and an "exploited." Anyone can see the fallacy in this enduring viewpoint: the willingness and even eagerness to trade suggests that both parties are bound to benefit. In modern game-theory language, trade is a win-win situation, a "positive-sum" rather than a "zero-sum" or "negative-sum" game. John has no food but he has money. That is why food has value to him. The grocer has lots of food but needs money, and therefore the money that John offers is of value to him.

How can a transaction be zero-sum? Many folks would cite taxation. If John pays a certain amount in taxes to the government but has no perception of receiving something of equal value, then he has the feeling that he's been exploited. It's up to the government to either do a better job of explaining to John how he has benefitted ("We stopped an invasion by the dictator next door, which was a good thing for you") or reduce his taxes.

On a larger scale, free market economies are characterized by the formation of complex transactional networks that produce and distribute goods and services throughout the economy. These networks are not consciously designed; rather they emerge as a result of decentralized individual economic decisions. The idea of spontaneous order is an elaboration on the invisible hand proposed by Adam Smith in *The Wealth of Nations*. Smith describes the free market trader:

"By preferring the support of domestic to that of foreign industry, he intends only his own security; and by directing that industry in such a manner as its produce may be of the greatest value, he intends only his own gain, and he is in this, as in many other cases, led by an invisible hand to promote an end which was no part of his intention. Nor is it always the worse for society that it was no part of it. By pursuing his own interest, [an individual] frequently promotes that of the society more effectually than when he really intends to promote it. I have never known much good done by those who affected to trade for the [common] good."

Smith pointed out that one does not get one's dinner by appealing to the charitable impulse of the butcher, the farmer, or the baker. Rather, one appeals to their self-interest, and pays them for their labor or product:

"It is not from the benevolence of the butcher, the brewer or the baker, that we expect our dinner, but from their regard to their own self-interest. We address ourselves, not to their humanity but to their self-love, and never talk to them of our own necessities but of their advantages."

It stands to reason that a hundred intelligent individuals, each choosing rationally what will benefit him or her, both in the short-term and the long-term, will make better decisions than a handful of master planners who in fact may have no personal stake in the outcomes of their decisions. This spontaneous order is superior to any contrived order that does not allow individuals to make their own choices of what to produce, what to buy, what to sell, and at what prices, due to the number and complexity of the factors involved. Central planning too often results in more disorder and the less efficient production and distribution of goods and services.

An individual is capable of thinking this: "Everywhere I go I see wheat offered for sale. Because the supply is so great, wheat has little value. On the other hand, corn is in short supply. People will pay a high price for corn because the supply is inadequate. Therefore, I'll grow corn. If I sell corn, I'll be doing a service to the community and I will also enrich myself. It's a win-win proposition." A government planner is much less likely to take such an objective viewpoint. Because the government planner isn't actually buying corn, he or she has no stake in the corn market. The problem remains an abstraction, not a reality.

The world didn't always have free markets. For endless centuries of human existence, societies and economies were organized around rigid caste systems. Kings ruled their kingdoms. Lords of the manor ruled their vast landed estates, which were lands granted to them by the king, wrestled from other lords, or handed down through generations. Eager partners in the caste system were the men of religion, who guarded the secrets of literacy and science.

Beneath them were the merchants and tradesmen. These were the makers of goods and the buyers and sellers of goods. These were people who passed on both their name and occupation to their children: Baker, butcher, carpenter, cooper, smith, and many others.

For centuries the land was farmed, used for grazing or hunting, but otherwise unimproved and unexploited. No factories, no productive labor force.

At the bottom were the serfs. For the lords who owned the land they grew crops and tended herds, and were allowed to keep only enough food for subsistence living.

Everyone knew their respective places. You were identified by the clothing that you wore. There was no social mobility. Serfs didn't rise to become merchants or tradesmen. Merchants or tradesmen didn't become lords. Lords didn't become kings. There was little progress or improvement in the standard of living because no one believed in the concept of being able to change their lot in life through invention and industry. Because serfs were forced to produce for lords, they had no interest in technological innovation. Because lords were not producing to sell on the market, there was no competitive pressure for them to innovate. Feudal manors were almost entirely self-sufficient, and therefore had no need for an active market. Trade was for the purpose of acquiring luxury goods such as silk and spices. There was no incentive for anyone to do more than was necessary to maintain the status quo.

What spurred social progress was the end of feudalism, the discovery of the New World, and the emergence of free markets.

As individuals gained more freedom, human progress accelerated. By the seventeenth and early eighteenth centuries, the restive middle class began to think there was more to life than knowing their place. They acted out of self-interest. Many saw the opportunity to accomplish something no one else had ever done—rise above their stations.

With rapid improvements in travel technology, middle class merchants and tradesmen soon became entrepreneurs. They saw the opportunities that economic freedom (or at least relatively more freedom) could offer and they took advantage of it. First came mercantilism, the system of trade for profit under which commodities were still largely produced by non-capitalist production methods. Progress accelerated as the Industrial Revolution took hold in England and then throughout Europe.

The Rise of Capitalism

In the mid-eighteenth century a new group of economic theorists, led by Adam Smith, challenged fundamental mercantilist doctrines as the belief that the amount of the world's wealth remained constant and that a state could only increase its wealth at the expense of another state. This period gave rise to industrial capitalism, made possible by the accumulation of vast amounts of capital under the merchant phase of capitalism and its investment in machinery. Industrial capitalism marked the development of the factory system of manufacturing, characterized by a complex division of labor between and within work processes and the standardization of work tasks; and finally established the global domination of the capitalist mode of production.

During the resulting Industrial Revolution, the industrialist replaced the merchant as a dominant actor in the capitalist system and hastened the decline of the traditional handicraft skills of artisans, guilds, and journeymen. Capitalism marked the transformation of relations between the land owning gentry and peasants, giving rise to the production of cash crops for the market rather than for subsistence on a feudal manor. The surplus generated by the rise of commercial agriculture encouraged the increased mechanization of agriculture.

Swift sailing vessels—the steam engine—the internal combustion engine—the telegraph—the electric light—the telephone—the radio—the list goes on and on, and the creative breakthroughs piled up on each other at an increasingly faster rate.

None of it, not one of these innovations, inventions, or improvements was created by an act of parliament or ministerial decree. They were created by entrepreneurs through ceaseless trial and error. The Industrial Revolution and its successor, the Communications Revolution, were the creations of human activity and ingenuity. They certainly weren't about governments planning progress.

By virtue of a vast supply of raw materials combined with a fluid social order in which anyone could attain wealth, the United States became a shining example of the success of free markets. The nation progressed from being a relatively minor industrial power in the mid-nineteenth century to becoming the most powerful economy on earth a scant one hundred years later.

The power of free market innovation, when unleashed, is incomparable. And the beauty of it is that a free market system need not be present from the very formation of a nation or society; a free market system can work wonders when introduced at any stage of an economy.

Margaret Thatcher and the United Kingdom

Where can we find an example of a large-scale national application of free market principles where previously there were suffocating government controls? Some would point to China, which in the past decade has loosened the iron grip of state control over many aspects of the lives of its citizens. But the state remains a heavy and ominous presence, especially in politics.

There exists a clearer and more dramatic example.

In the late 1970s, England was not a good place to live. The 1978-79 Winter of Discontent was marked by public sector strikes that left rubbish piled high in the streets and the dead unburied. By 1979, when Margaret Thatcher became prime minister, the British polity was in a mess. Inflation and unemployment were rising and the unions seemed to be unstoppable. The glorious days when the sun never set on the British Empire seemed like a faded relic of the past, never to be repeated. The Union Jack had become a tattered remnant of its former self.

In contrast to her immediate predecessors at Number 10 Downing Street, Margaret Thatcher's political philosophy and economic policies emphasized deregulation of the financial and industrial sectors, flexible labor markets, the privatization of state-owned companies, and a sharp reduction in the power and influence of trade unions. The process of privatization, especially the preparation of nationalized industries for privatization, was associated with marked improvements in performance, particularly in terms of labor productivity.

Against all conventional wisdom, Thatcher took an ax to public spending. In 1979 Deputy Prime Minister Geoffrey Howe abolished Britain's exchange controls, allowing more capital to be invested in foreign markets, and the Big Bang of 1986 removed many restrictions on the London Stock Exchange. The Thatcher government encouraged growth in the finance and service sectors to compensate for Britain's ailing manufacturing industry.

Thatcher was committed to reducing the power of the trade unions, whose leadership she accused of undermining parliamentary democracy and economic performance through strike action. Several unions launched strikes in response to legislation introduced to curb their power, but resistance eventually collapsed.

Thatcher battled to "roll back the frontiers of the state." Privatization began with National Freight and was extended to include steel, gas, telecoms, and water. State support for private industry was phased out. Local authority homes were sold to tenants at a discount, dramatically boosting home ownership, though at the cost of an enduring gap in housing provision for the poor.

In the short term, the economic medicine was not easy for many to swallow. Unemployment rose above three million, manufacturing output fell, and the new prime minister's poll rating went south. At one celebrated meeting she even demanded an extra one billion pounds cut in spite of warnings from those present that the country would fall apart. Resisting calls for a softer line, she told the 1980 Conservative conference: "To those waiting for the favorite media catchphrase 'the U-turn', I have only one thing to say: You turn if you want to. The lady's not for turning."

The free market policies slowly worked. In 1983, inflation was down below four per cent from a peak of twenty-two per cent. Years later, Lord Carrington, who became her foreign secretary, said: "Her finest hour really was with the economy and changing people's perceptions of what we ought to be doing." Her election victory in 1983, against a Labour party led by the elderly Michael Foot, was a shoo-in.

If Britain's military triumph in the Falkland Islands was the most dramatic event of her first term, the defeat on a peacetime battlefield of the National Union of Mineworkers was the outstanding victory of her second. The miner's strike was a bloody conflict with communities torn apart and pitched battles between miners and the police. Yet the NUM, previously seen as invincible by any government, was eventually forced to retreat.

By 1987, unemployment was falling, the economy was stable and strong, and inflation was low.

These advances towards a more open domestic economy began to appear unstoppable. Thatcher hated any idea of a wider European superstate. In an outspoken 1988 speech in Bruges, she insisted: "We haven't worked all these years to free Britain from the paralysis of socialism only to see it creep in through the back door of central control and bureaucracy from Brussels."

Despite her eventual political isolation and fall from power, by unleashing the power of free markets Margaret Thatcher reversed decades of decline and set Great Britain on a new course of prosperity and leadership.

The Transformation of Sweden

Great Britain is not the only nation to have benefited from a good dose of free market medicine.

In 1968 England's neighbor to the northeast, Sweden, was the world's third richest country in per capita gross domestic product. (The United States and Kuwait occupied the first and second slots, respectively. The United Kingdom limped in at number twenty, after Finland.) Life was very good indeed.

That changed very quickly. In the 1970s and 1980s Sweden could claim world leadership in government-managed economics in the mold of John Maynard Keynes, with a ninety percent marginal tax rate and a welfare state second to none. It became a prototype for how not to run an economy. According to a 2012 study from the Research Institute of Industrial Economics, Sweden slid to number seventeen in the global income rankings. From 1970 until 1989, taxes rose exorbitantly, entitlements became excessive, and private initiative was stifled. Laws were byzantine and became unpredictable. As a consequence, Sweden endured two decades of mediocre growth. In 1991-93, the country suffered a severe crash in real estate and banking that reduced gross domestic product by six percent. In 1993 public spending had surged to 71.7 percent of GDP, and the budget deficit reached eleven percent of GDP.

After the Keynesian financial and monetary stimulus in the 1970s and '80s, which led to inflation, repeated devaluations, and low growth, Swedes came to believe in fiscal discipline. They became averse to huge national debt and budget deficits, especially at the levels seen in many other countries.

The turnaround began under Prime Minister Carl Bildt. From 1991 to 1994 his government policies focused on liberalizing and reforming the Swedish economy and making Sweden a member of the European Union. Economic reforms were enacted including voucher schools, liberalizing markets for telecommunications and energy, and privatizing publicly owned companies and health care.

In 1994, the Social Democrats returned to power and stayed until 2006. During their tenure they completed the fiscal tightening. In 2006, a non-socialist government returned, and since then Finance Minister Anders Borg, with his distinctive ponytail and earring, has led further reforms. An incremental dismantling of the social democratic welfare state, with larger self-financing of welfare systems, lower taxes, and fewer benefits were seen as the way to create new motivation to work, more business opportunities, and more jobs.

Sweden's traditional bane has been taxes, which used to be the highest in the world. The current government has cut them every year and abolished wealth taxes. Inheritance and gift taxes are also gone. Until 1990, the maximum marginal income tax rate was ninety percent. As of this writing it is 56.5 percent. That is still one of the world's highest, and there is strong public support for a cut to fifty percent. The twenty-six percent tax on corporate profits may seem reasonable from an American perspective, but Swedish business leaders want to reduce it to twenty percent.

The annual centralized wage bargaining between the Trade Union Confederation and the Swedish Employers' Confederation, which in the 1970s led to both inflation and strikes, is gone. Wage bargaining is still collective, but it is decentralized. Wage inflation is no longer a concern and strikes are extremely rare. Employers have been unshackled, but wages are rising with productivity, so the workers are benefiting as well. As of everywhere, trade unions are losing members, money, and power.

During this current century, the country has been reformed. Public spending has fallen by no less than one-fifth of gross domestic product, markets have opened up, and taxes have dropped. Current data from the International Monetary Fund and the Organization for Economic Cooperation and Development show that Sweden has one of the lowest inflation rates in Europe. It runs a budget surplus every year, its corporate tax rates are considerably lower than US rates, and as a share of its economy it spends more on research and development than the United States. Its firms are highly competitive in the world economy, and it runs sizable current-account surpluses.

The union economists, who dominated Swedish economic debate in the 1970s and '80s, have been replaced by bank economists. The new values are competition, openness, and efficiency, while social and environmental values remain. This has resulted in a social-welfare society without the social-welfare state. The idea is to make the economy more efficient through competition among private providers. Sweden is still offering good social welfare, but is doing so more efficiently and sensibly, and increasingly through the private sector. This model of falling taxes and public spending is rapidly proliferating from the north of Europe toward the south.

Hong Kong: A Shining Star of Free Trade

Imagine a laboratory experiment in which there was established within a well-defined geographic region a zone of free enterprise. The salient conditions would be free trade, low income and business taxes, and minimal government intervention. The performance of the economy could be gauged over time. How would such a place fare? Would there be anarchy? Would greedy people cheat each other? Or would the place prosper and bustle with productive activity?

The experiment has been done and is thriving today. Anyone can go there and see the results.

Situated on China's south coast, Hong Kong has a long history as a center of trade. With a land mass covering a scant 426 square miles and a population of seven million people, Hong Kong is one of the most densely populated areas in the world. The lack of space has resulted in highly compact urban construction, which developed the city into a center for modern architecture and the world's most vertical metropolis. The territory has little arable land and few natural resources, so it imports most of its food and raw materials. Agricultural activity—relatively unimportant to Hong Kong's economy and contributing just 0.1 percent of its GDP—primarily consists of growing premium food and flower varieties.

Since the British relinquished control in 1997, this city-state has been one of the two Special Administrative Regions of the People's Republic of China. Hong Kong Basic Law, its constitutional document, stipulates that Hong Kong shall have a "high degree of autonomy" in all matters except foreign relations and military defense.

As one of the world's leading international financial centers, Hong Kong has a major capitalist service economy characterized by low taxation and free trade. Every year since 1995, its economy has been ranked the freest in the world by the Index of Economic Freedom. It's an important center for international finance and trade, with one of the greatest concentrations of corporate headquarters in the Asia-Pacific region.

Hong Kong is a free port that thrives on free trade. Its open door policy has enabled it to become one of the world's largest trading economies and an international financial and commercial center serving the Asia-Pacific region and the Mainland of China.

The cornerstone of this approach is a strong and credible multilateral trading system. The World Trade Organization (WTO), which came into being in 1995 to succeed the General Agreement on Tariffs and Trade (GATT), provides strengthened rules and disciplines for the conduct of multilateral trade. Hong Kong is a founding member of the WTO and participates in its activities. Since July 1, 1997, Hong Kong has continued its separate membership using the name "Hong Kong, China."

The free trade policy means Hong Kong maintains no barriers on trade. Thus, Hong Kong does not charge a tariff on the importation or exportation of goods. Import and export licensing is also kept to a minimum. Licensing is only imposed when there is a genuine need to fulfill obligations undertaken by Hong Kong to its trading partners, or to meet public health, safety, or internal security needs.

Hong Kong was once described by Milton Friedman as the world's greatest experiment in laissez-faire capitalism, but has since instituted a regime of regulations including a minimum wage. And yes, there are taxes to be paid. In Hong Kong, personal tax is often referred to as salary tax. Both corporate and personal tax rates in Hong Kong are considered to be among the lowest in the world. Unlike a flat corporate tax rate, Hong Kong's salary tax rates follow a progressive tax rate system. As of this writing, there are four marginal tax brackets of two percent, seven percent, twelve percent, and seventeen percent. Individuals are taxed at progressive rates on their net chargeable income (i.e. assessable income after deductions and allowances) starting at two percent and ending at seventeen percent; or at a standard rate of fifteen percent on net income (i.e. income after deductions), whichever is lower.

There is no capital gains tax, no dividend tax, and no inheritance tax.

Positive Non-Interventionism

While it follows a free market model, Hong Kong is not an ungoverned frontier town. Positive non-interventionism has long been the economic policy of the government of Hong Kong; this policy can be traced back to the time when the island was under British rule. It was first officially implemented in 1971 by John Cowperthwaite, who observed that the economy was doing well in the absence of government intervention but it was important to create the regulatory and physical infrastructure to facilitate market-based decision making. The policy was continued by subsequent financial secretaries, including Sir Philip Haddon-Cave. The government has intervened to create economic institutions such as the Hong Kong Stock Market, and has been involved in public works projects and social welfare spending.

By any standard, the measurable results continue to be impressive.

• Hong Kong has one of the highest per capita incomes in the world.

• According to estimates from both the United Nations and the World Health Organization, Hong Kong had the longest life expectancy of any region in the world in 2012.

• Between 1961 and 1997 Hong Kong's gross domestic product grew 180 times while per capita GDP increased eighty-seven times over.

• Hong Kong is ranked fourth in terms of the highest percentage of millionaire households, behind Switzerland, Qatar, and Singapore with 8.5 percent of all households owning at least one million US dollars.

• In 2011, Hong Kong was ranked second in the Ease of Doing Business Index, behind Singapore.

• According to the Index of Economic Freedom, since the inception of the index in 1995, Hong Kong has remained as the world's freest economy.

• As of 2012, Hong Kong women are the longest living demographic group in the world.

• Gross domestic product (GDP) per capita at purchasing power parity was the sixth highest globally in 2011, more than the United States and the Netherlands, and slightly lower than the Brunei.

Low levels of spending relative to GDP (for example, no spending on armed forces, minimal outlays for foreign affairs and modest recurrent social welfare spending) have allowed the accumulation of very large fiscal reserves with minimal foreign debt.

Could the example of Hong Kong be replicated anywhere in the world? No; it's a relatively uncomplicated city-state that is free of many of the social, historical, and geographic challenges that burden other places. Without its spectacular deepwater port, Hong Kong might just as well be another overcrowded coastal village. But the example of Hong Kong's enduring economic success should stand as a reminder that the free market system is a powerful force for good.

Why Free Markets Work

What is it about the power of free markets that is transformative? A free market is regarded by many leading economists and politicians as the purest and most effective model for organizing economic activity between producers and consumers. Because it is driven by efficiency that leads to increased profits, a free market produces the most goods or services at the lowest possible price. This means that the maximum number of people can use the goods or services, which increases the standard of living (or, in the case of disasters, can save lives). In a free market, consumers seek to pay the lowest possible price, which reduces the cost of living.

That is not to say that free markets are always perfect. They are not. But unlike most centrally planned enterprises, a free market will quickly right itself. The farmer who grows wheat one year has the choice to grow corn the next year if he or she thinks that corn is in short supply. The principle of a free market means that no individual or small group controls the price, and that any potential to meet a demand by selling a good or service will be met by one competitor or another.

It's true that this principle can break down if there are not enough sellers or buyers. For example, the US government greatly dominates the purchase of all military equipment, thus skewing the forces of a free market. Monopolies or oligarchies operate at a distance from true free markets with perfect competition, and reduce the benefits that society might have achieved otherwise.

The reality is that in today's global economy, most markets are not perfectly free. Many of them are close enough so that free-market-like behavior dominates even though the specifics fail the test at one or more points. It should also be made clear that laissez-faire or totally unregulated markets often fall short in creating a beneficial, economically free market. Truly free and effective markets depend on certain social institutions like fair and independent courts and other forms of ensuring every participant plays by the rules. They do not necessarily arise organically on their own. Property rights, contract law, and trade law have evolved to the extent that they are now being readily adopted by countries wanting to rapidly construct a legal platform for growth.

Free Markets Create New Technologies

The example of the individual farmer who chooses to plant corn instead of wheat and therefore contributes to the common good holds true in many areas of life including technology. While it is true that governments sponsor important technological research—atomic energy is a prime example—in a free market system there are countless independent actors who relentlessly identify problems and try to solve them. Sometimes the solutions don't work. But that's okay, because if one solution fails, other inventors are toiling away at other solutions that might succeed. Thus, progress is made incrementally, by trial and error, testing and refining.

Here are two recent examples of innovation in the energy sector.

The HVDC Circuit Breaker

One of the biggest issues facing renewable energy is that few users live where wind power can consistently generate electricity, such as on mountaintops or on the oceans far offshore. But electricity can be transported to where it's needed, and the electricity that is generated in these remote locations could be converted to high voltage direct current (HVDC) and carried long distances on HVDC lines. They are cheaper to operate and more efficient conductors than AC transmission lines.

A barrier to deploying this type of technology has been the lack of a HVDC circuit breaker, which is a critical component in a stable and safe grid. HVDC circuit breakers are difficult to build because some mechanism must be included in the circuit breaker to force the current to zero, otherwise arcing and contact wear would be too great to allow reliable switching.

There can be no doubt that around the world there have been many inventors, from solitary tinkerers in their garages to big corporations with well-funded R&D departments, who have worked on this problem. In 2012 the ABB Group, an energy technology company based in Zurich, announced that they had invented a practical HVDC breaker. "ABB has written a new chapter in the history of electrical engineering," said Joe Hogan, chief executive of ABB, in a report in *The Guardian*. "HVDC technology is needed to facilitate the long distance transfer of power from hydropower plants, the integration of offshore wind power, the development of visionary solar projects, and the interconnection of different power networks. This historical breakthrough will make it possible to build the grid of the future."

Was ABB motivated by self-interest? Of course; they hope to sell their products at a profit. But a significant consequence of their effort is that humans are one step closer to developing large scale renewable energy sources that will benefit everyone.

The GravityLight

In another example of the endless problems that vex mankind, one of the great afflictions of the very poor is the absence of electric lights. According to the World Bank, over 1.2 billion people—twenty percent of the world's population—are without access to electricity worldwide. Almost all of them live in developing countries. This includes about

550 million people in Africa and over 400 million in India. Those who lack this necessity of life that is taken for granted in industrialized nations must use kerosene lamps, candles, or oil lamps to see at night. By using open flames they risk burns, jeopardize their respiratory health, and increase their risk of cancer. The World Bank estimates that 780 million women and children inhale household smoke that is the equivalent to smoking two packs of cigarettes every day. Sixty percent of adult female lung cancer victims in developing nations are non-smokers. The fumes also cause eye infections and cataracts. The very poor often must spend a significant proportion of their income on kerosene, and all of those open flames add carbon dioxide to the atmosphere.

The increasing availability and decreasing price of LED lights has the potential to change this equation. But in terms of electricity supply, most people who live far from the grid have no money to pay for the solar cells and battery storage systems that power solar lighting. Inexpensive lamps with self-contained batteries are low powered and have a limited battery life. People cannot afford ongoing maintenance and support of larger systems, so solar lighting becomes a project for communities rather than individual households. In short, solar may not always be the best solution for lighting the homes of people on very low incomes.

A project by a London-based industrial design company by the name of therefore.com devised a radical solution. GravityLight is a lamp powered by a bag of sand or rocks suspended on a pulley, like the weights on a grandfather clock. As the bag descends it powers a tiny generator that lights the LEDs. After about a half-hour, you reset the device by pulling up the bag, which weighs about twenty pounds. As each unit is fully self-contained, there are no solar cells to gather energy from the sun and no expensive batteries in which to store energy. Because there are no operating costs after the initial low cost purchase, it has the potential to lift people out of poverty, allowing them to use the money they have saved to buy more powerful solar lighting systems in the future.

The company hopes to be able to sell it for five or ten dollars, which is a fraction of the cost of an equivalent solar powered lamp. Funding for the project was provided in part by an Indiegogo crowdfunding campaign. The initial goal was $55,000, and the campaign raised $399,590 from 6,219 funders.

The BioLite Stove

The lack of electricity in developing nations means that households not only do not have electric lights, but they also must cook with a fuel burning stove. In low-income households, biomass fuel is available and is much cheaper than fuels like gas. Burning biomass—wood, dung, or plant material—for cooking in enclosed spaces creates smoke pollution. Smoke pollution from traditional cooking stoves is a major threat to child health in Africa today, and is thought to be a major trigger of fatal infant pneumonia in thousands of African children each year. The World Health Organization calls pneumonia the biggest global killer of children under five, more so than malaria, tuberculosis, and even AIDS.

At a workshop in Dumbo, Brooklyn, a team of entrepreneurs is refining the BioLite stove, an invention designed to dramatically cut smoke emissions. The new BioLite stove, by virtue of its smoke-reducing burn, should diminish—and conceivably could eradicate—the threat from smoke pollution.

Invented by Alexander Drummond and Jonathan Cedar, the stove itself is a fifteen-pound, hourglass-shaped silver-colored appliance that comes up to a height of your knees. It has become the connection between its trendy Brooklyn-based designers and a group of academics at Columbia University. The latter, who are pollution epidemiologists, have tested versions of the BioLite stove in pilot trials on four continents, which yielded results positive enough to generate funding for a five-year long trial in Ghana, West Africa. "The country's political stability made it the easiest place to expand the project", said primary researcher Patrick Kinney, who works at Columbia's Mailman School of Public Health.

The BioLite stove decreases smokiness by ninety-four percent and just about eliminates black carbon. Researchers believe that if most of the visible smoke is gone, then the threat will go with it too; a hypothesis that will be tested in the large-scale trial. In traditional cooking fire set-ups, plumes of smoke escape from beneath the cooking pot and turn the air toxic. The BioLite burns wood more efficiently so that it releases almost no smoke. This is important because smoke indicates that some of the fuel is not being used, escaping instead in a form that is toxic. No smoke means that just about all of the fuel gets burnt.

As a bonus, an attachment on the side of the unit gathers waste heat and converts it into electricity, reducing smoke emissions while simultaneously providing users with the capability to charge mobile phones and LED lights. In addition, because the BioLite home stove uses fuel efficiently, you have to use less fuel. Even though biomass fuel is cheaper than kerosene, the average impoverished family in the Third World spends up to thirty percent of their income on fuel, compared with only four percent in the United States.

The BioLite stove technology was inspired by a philosophy of applying efficient design to real world problems. According to the BioLite website, Drummond and Cedar met at the design consultancy Smart Design in New York City, where they quickly bonded over their interest in sustainable design in 2006. Drummond, frustrated that all efficient camping stoves required petroleum fuel or batteries, had the idea of a wood-burning stove able to utilize its own thermal energy. Cedar, an avid camper, quickly brought his engineering background to the table and the two began the design process. Countless nights, weekends, and prototypes later, the first BioLite stove was born.

The PlayPump

While electricity and fuel are important for human survival, no less important is access to clean water. In nearly every part of the developing world, and at the scene of many a natural disaster, access to clean drinkable water is a huge problem.

Roughly one third of all nations suffer from clean water scarcity. According to Water.org, more than 3.4 million people die each year from water, sanitation, and hygiene-related causes. Ninety-nine percent of these deaths occur in the developing world. Lack of access to clean water and sanitation kills children at a rate equivalent to a jumbo jet crashing every four hours. Of the sixty million people added to the world's towns and cities every year, most move to sprawling urban slums with no sanitation facilities. Approximately one in nine people on earth are without an improved water source.

Of any inhabited place on the globe, Sub-Saharan Africa has the largest number of water-stressed countries, where three hundred million live with a severe water deficit. According to findings presented at the 2012 Conference on Water Scarcity in Africa: Issues and Challenges, it is estimated that by 2030, seventy-five million to two hundred and fifty million people in Africa will be living in areas of high water stress, which will likely displace anywhere between twenty-four million and seven hundred million people as conditions become increasingly unlivable.

The costs to public health are enormous. Those living in water deprived regions must turn to unsafe water resources, which, according to the World Health Organization, directly contribute to the spread of waterborne diseases including malaria, typhoid fever, cholera, dysentery, and diarrhea, and can lead to diseases such as trachoma, plague, and typhus. Water scarcity forces many people to store water within the household, which increases the risk of household water contamination and incidents of malaria and dengue fever spread by mosquitoes.

To address this crisis, entrepreneurs around the world have been striving to develop simple technologies that can access and store underground water sources.

One such innovation is the PlayPump water system. Manufactured by the South African company Roundabout Outdoor, it's an almost ridiculously simple idea. The unit consists of a children's playground merry-go-round that's attached to a water pump. It operates in a similar way to a windmill-driven water pump. As children play on the merry-go-round, the spinning motion pumps underground water into a 2,500-liter tank raised seven meters above ground. The water in the tank is dispensed by a tap valve. According to the manufacturer, the pump can raise up to 1,400 liters of water per hour from a depth of forty meters. Excess water is diverted below ground again.

The storage tank has a four-sided advertising panel. Two sides are used to advertise products, thereby providing money for maintenance of the pump, and the other two sides are devoted to public health messages about topics like HIV/AIDS prevention. The PlayPump offers not only clean water but potentially life-saving messages that can help prevent the spread of the virus. The PlayPump won a World Bank Development Marketplace Award in 2000 for its effectiveness both at pumping water and communicating HIV/AIDS messages through billboards on the water towers.

The PlayPump is not the cheapest solution. At a cost of approximately US$14,000 each, the device is suitable for primary schools, particularly in areas where water is accessed from deep underground using a bore. According to the company, the cost covers not only the equipment, but also visiting the site to ensure the school understands and accepts the PlayPump, and testing of the borehole water to make sure it is sustainable. The water is sent to a recognized laboratory to make sure it is fit for human consumption. The installation is carried out by trained installers and the cost of getting the equipment to the site is covered in the cost. All spare parts are supplied free of charge.

Apart from the health benefits to the community of clean, easily accessible drinking water and the recreation opportunities given to the children, the PlayPump allows children to spend more time in school instead of hauling water, and enables women who formerly had to carry large containers of water over great distances to spend more time at home or engaged in other activities that provide additional food or income to their families.

Are the devices perfect? No. In fact, during the few years of field use there were significant problems. PlayPumps cost four times what a regular water pump does. Aid workers reported that they broke and were hard to fix. Critics said that children would have to play on the device around the clock to meet PlayPumps' originally stated target of providing 2,500 people per pump with their daily water needs. The PlayPump can reasonably supply drinking water in the amount of two liters, per child, per day. The United Nations World Water Assessment Programme (WWAP) suggests that every human being needs between twenty and fifty liters of water a day to ensure their basic needs for drinking, cooking, and cleaning are met. Even on the low end of the scale, the PlayPump is not going to provide all the water needed for the users. A crucial adaptation of the PlayPump model was Water For People's guarantee that the PlayPump would never serve as the sole provider of water for an entire community—the school and all the households surrounding it.

In 2009, the Case Foundation—an early funder of the project—released its own criticisms of the project.

"After three years of working on the ground in Africa," wrote CEO Jean Case, "PlayPumps has identified significant concerns related to maintenance of the pumps in certain areas. While the initiative has brought hundreds of new pumps to Africa—an outcome we celebrate—at the same time some mix of the scale and reach, combined with a downturn in the economy, has meant that local contractors can't keep pace with the maintenance needs. It is becoming clear that the kind of scale we hoped for will not likely be achievable in the timeframes initially outlined. As a result, Gary Edson, a strong leader with both development and business expertise, was brought on board as CEO of PlayPumps International to help the organization take a hard look at the right ways to go forward with humanitarian efforts in the future and how to best take and apply lessons learned from our involvement to date."

The foundation pivoted its programming, de-emphasizing the flashy technology and instead focusing on a specific outcome: clean water for children in schools. This led to the installation of more effective, government-approved technologies in schools, thus allowing children to focus on learning rather than pumping water all day.

The development, testing, and deployment of the PlayPump is an ongoing effort. In the spring of 2013 a new PlayPump was installed at the Tshwarelela Primary School in the city of Kimberley, capital of the Northern Cape Province in South Africa, as part of a clean water collaboration between Itron, Inc. (a company that delivers advanced metering infrastructure and automated meter reading solutions to help water providers better manage and conserve precious water resources) and its customer, Kimberley's Sol Plaatje Municipality.

The pilot project between Itron and the local municipality is the first of its kind in South Africa, and Itron is currently exploring additional sites for investment.

The PlayPump was officially opened on Friday, April 12, 2013 by the executive mayor of Sol Plaatje, Agnes Ntlhangula, and other council officials. The excitement of the 1,250 Tshwarelela Primary School students was evident as they gathered in the square to sing and dance nearly two hours before the official ribbon cutting.

Itron donated the PlayPump to Tshwarelela Primary School and will provide ongoing maintenance, dramatically reducing the school's water costs and enabling the school to reallocate funds to student programs. Access to this free water also enables the expansion of the school's vegetable garden into a community garden that allows residents to grow food and help the community.

The important question for any community is whether the PlayPump is worth the price tag. Is it cheaper than the alternative, which is for people to walk miles to access potentially unsafe water? That's a question that can be answered only by individual communities. For some places the PlayPump may be cost effective, while for others it may not.

Meanwhile, development continues. That's the beauty of the free market system. Put an idea out there, test it, improve it, and see where it leads. Then go back to the drawing board and improve it again.

LifeStraw

If you Google "clean water invention," you'll get dozens of fascinating ideas. One of the most well-known is the LifeStraw personal water filter, a "Best Invention of the Year" winner in *Time* magazine. The simple tube enables users to drink water safely from contaminated water sources. Lightweight and compact, LifeStraw is designed to be used during emergencies such as local flooding, which can contaminate drinking water supplies. It's also ideal for campers and hikers who may be drinking from rivers or lakes and are unsure of the water safety. Since 2005, LifeStraw has been used in developing countries to assist in achieving the United Nations' Millennium Development Goals for clean drinking water.

According to the manufacturer, Swiss-based Vestergaard Frandsen, LifeStraw surpasses EPA guidelines for E. coli, Giardia, and Cryptosporidium oocysts. It filters up to one thousand liters (264 gallons) of water, removes 99.9999% of waterborne bacteria (>LOG 6 reduction), and removes 99.9% of waterborne protozoan parasites (>LOG 3 reduction).

Designed for people living in developing nations and for distribution in humanitarian crisis, the larger LifeStraw Family filters a maximum of 18,000 liters of water, providing safe drinking water for a family of five for up to three years. Although LifeStraw is available for retail sale in the developing world, the majority of LifeStraws are distributed as part of public health campaigns or in response to complex emergencies by NGOs and organizations that give them away for free in the developing world. Both LifeStraw and LifeStraw Family were distributed in the 2010 Haiti earthquake, 2010 Pakistan floods, and 2011 Thailand floods. In the Mutomo District in Kenya, which has suffered from long-term drought, the Kenya Red Cross supplied filters to 3,750 school children and 6,750 households.

Life Cube

The preceding examples illustrate technologies that can be used on a long-term basis, not just for immediate disaster relief. As we have seen in earthquake disasters, very often the immediate short-term needs are for food, water, and shelter. The latter is particularly challenging because shelters designed for human habitation, even on a short-term basis, are large objects that require substantial manufacturing and transport costs.

There's a market space between those infamous long-term FEMA trailers and the flimsy tents often used in the immediate recovery efforts. In FEMA's 2008 Disaster Housing Plan, officials identified the period as being after the initial disaster, but before homes can be rebuilt as a major priority. "Finding and providing the actual structures to house displaced disaster victims during this interim housing period is the most tangible challenge that emergency management officials, at all levels of government, face," FEMA wrote. In developing countries, providing basic shelter after disasters is even more difficult. When a major quake struck Pakistan in October 2005, 74,000 people died, most of them from exposure to the elements in the weeks after the initial disaster.

Established in 2009 and based in Santa Barbara, California, Life Cube, Inc. is a specialist in rapid deployment shelter technologies. The genesis of the Life Cube shelter began when entrepreneur Michael Conner witnessed the devastation in 2005 wrought by Hurricane Katrina as well as the massive earthquake in Pakistan. Watching humanitarian efforts, it became clear to him that a quickly deployable, portable shelter could be enormously helpful in providing life-saving shelter and supporting on-the-ground operations by aid workers.

Conner immediately committed himself to invent an entirely new class of transportable shelter—one that would combine the ruggedness and utility of a trailer with the speed and expandability of breakthrough inflatable technology. The result is the Life Cube. Today, Life Cube, Inc. is a leading designer, manufacturer and distributor of innovative air-beam shelters for a variety of markets and uses.

The Life Cube shelter arrives in a four-foot-square crate made from post-consumer recycled plastic shipping pallets. Integrated into the crate are steel hoops that make it possible to roll the cube along the ground. Upon arrival to a safe location, the plastic pallets are opened and laid on the ground in a square, with an extra for the entrance pad. Then, a CO_2 canister included with the package inflates the twelve-foot-high canopy, which is manufactured by the Patten Company, who has made US Navy life rafts for over fifty years. The inflatable canopy is made from polyester fabric that is tear-proof and fire-retardant and designed to withstand winds up to fifty miles per hour. Life Cube offers one hundred and forty-four square feet of instant emergency space and requires no tools to set up. There are three doors, which allow multiple shelters to be lined up and zipped together creating multiple rooms.

Among Life Cube's standard features are a self-sufficient, solar powered power system, communications equipment, water filtration devices, propane or kerosene cook top, first aid kits, ready-to-eat meals (MREs), and a wide variety of essential survival supplies. Completely US-made, each Life Cube is manufactured and assembled entirely in Florida and California.

"We need a versatile design that is completely self-contained that gives you instant survival," said Nick Pedersen, business development head of the startup, in *Wired* magazine. "We'll get you through the critical first seventy-two hours and beyond."

Is the Life Cube the answer to the problem of providing emergency shelter after a disaster? Perhaps, yes; perhaps, no. But it's a good start, and an imperfect solution is better than no solution. The free market of ideas will be the judge. Real-world testing will reveal both flaws and strong points. Then the design will go back to the drawing board for improvements, and it will be tested again. That's how progress is made.

Tom's Shoes

As we have seen in the previous examples, innovation that is designed to uplift impoverished peoples often takes the form of a new invention that leverages the technologies that are appropriate to a particular culture or region. The people of the region use the invention or device and their lives are improved.

Sometimes innovation can take the form of a business model. That is, the benefit to an impoverished area comes from a side effect of a business model whose mission includes not only returning a profit to the owners but also delivering something of value at low cost or no cost to low-income peoples. The thing of value may be fairly ordinary, at least to people in industrialized nations, but is in short supply or is unaffordable to families who subsist on pennies a day.

A good example is shoes. For many reasons, one of which is outlined below, humans need to wear shoes. Because they wear out, shoes have a short life span and must be regularly replaced. Good shoes are not cheap, especially for people in poverty.

Wearing shoes is critical not just for comfort or style but for public and personal health. They provide significant protection against certain epidermal parasitic skin diseases (EPSDs), which occur worldwide and have been known since ancient times. Six EPSDs are of particular prevalence: scabies, three forms of pediculosis (head lice, body lice, and pubic lice infestation), tungiasis (sand flea disease), and hookworm-related cutaneous larva migrans (HrCLM). They are either common in resource-poor settings or are associated with important morbidity. The six major EPSDs differ considerably in their biological and epidemiological characteristics and life cycles.

Tungiasis is spread by sand fleas (*Tunga penetrans*). The parasite may persist for months and can cause long-lasting sequels. In its 2009 bulletin entitled "Epidermal parasitic skin diseases: a neglected category of poverty-associated plagues," the World Health Organization underlined the importance of shoes as a barrier to this destructive parasite:

"In resource-poor settings, stray dogs and cats are common and organic waste frequently litters the soil. Rats are attracted if garbage is not collected, sewage is not disposed of properly, and food is stored inadequately. The risk for infestation is high if feet are not protected by shoes and socks, either because people cannot afford them or if wearing shoes is not part of local custom. In resource-poor rural and indigenous populations in the hinterland of Brazil, the transmission of *T. penetrans* occurred almost exclusively indoors. Dwellings in these settings typically do not possess a solid floor, or the ground is covered with rough concrete or broken tiles with many crevices, thus providing an ideal habitat for the off-host development of *T. penetrans*. In an urban environment it spreads in slums, where roads and paths are not paved, waste litters the area and yards consist of sand or mud."

Shoes are a fairly easy commodity to manufacture; the world's factories churn out roughly twenty billion pairs of shoes every year (over half come from China). So, in theory, there should be enough shoes for every person on the planet, but that's not the case. The challenge is not supply but distribution. In some Western closets you'll see shoes lined up by the dozens, while in many Third World villages there's nary a shoe to be seen.

Founded in 2006 by Blake Mycoskie, an entrepreneur from Arlington, Texas, Toms is a for-profit shoe company based in Santa Monica, California, that operates the non-profit subsidiary, Friends of Toms. The company designs and sells shoes based on the Argentine alpargata design, as well as eyewear. When Toms sells one pair of shoes, another pair of shoes is given to an impoverished child. The company has become so closely identified with giving away a pair of shoes to a poor child for every pair sold—Toms has trademarked the tagline "one for one"—that it's often mistaken for a charity.

Toms currently donates shoes in fifty-nine countries and eyewear in thirteen. In the spring of 2013, Toms gave away its ten millionth pair of shoes. The figures add up to remarkable growth for a remarkable company, one that has put shoes on the feet of many poor children, made its owner a very wealthy man, and pioneered a much-admired business model. "I had no idea it would ever get this big," said Mycoskie in a profile by Jeff Chu in *Fast Company*. "Now that we've grown, it's all about: How do you use these resources to do even more?"

The privately owned company does not release revenue or profit figures. But Mycoskie told Chu that the average retail price for a pair of Toms is fifty-five dollars, and that about thirty percent of its revenues come from direct-to-consumer sales via its website, Toms.com. Analysts figure that Toms sells about seven million pairs of shoes annually, giving a gross income of nearly four hundred million dollars from the shoe business.

All of Toms' consumer shoes today are made in China, as are the vast majority of its giveaway shoes (a small number of which are distributed there). "Toms would not be what it is today without China," said Toms president Laurent Potdevin. "We wouldn't have the resources we have now. It has been the easiest, most cost-effective place to make shoes."

All of this sounds wonderful, but—perhaps not surprisingly—as the Toms shoe giveaway program grew the critics took aim. Some pointed out that by giving away free shoes, you don't do anything to alter the economy of an impoverished region. People may have new shoes but they still don't have jobs. Giving away shoes may even hurt local shoemakers and shoe sellers. It has been seen as the equivalent of "dumping," where a powerful manufacturer enters a market and wipes out competitors by selling its product at a loss.

In response, Toms began to make its giveaway shoes in Ethiopia, which has a small but thriving shoemaking sector. Toms expects to add shoemaking capabilities in India, Kenya, and Haiti. These efforts are not without their challenges. Potdevin said, "Getting a factory up and running, retention, training, finding local management—every aspect is more difficult in a place like Haiti." Additionally, the factories that Toms set up must conform to its social welfare standards by offering generous wages as well as benefits including tutoring for workers' children, financial education, company-provided take-home meals for working moms, and at a Kenyan factory an onsite preschool. On the other hand, if you're creating products destined for the local market, your distribution costs are much lower; no sea freight from China and no import tariffs. Staying local is especially important in Africa; Kenya and Ethiopia are both members of a free-trade zone that includes nearly every African country where Toms shoes are given away.

That's the free enterprise model: formulate the idea, test it in the field, get feedback and criticism, and make adjustments. It's nimble and responsive, and the focus is always on getting the job done.

Chapter Four: Pioneers in Radical Response

In this chapter, we're proud to present exclusive interviews with five free market proponents who have each in their own way spearheaded a radical response designed to uplift humanity.

Michael McCausland: Sustainable Communities Worldwide

Having traveled to more than 140 countries in the past twelve years, many of them the most socially, politically and financially challenged in the world, Michael McCausland has spent time in the trenches of poverty like only a very few of us have. His tasks have ranged from helping pick up the pieces of villages ravaged by guerilla soldiers raping and pillaging to organizing global training programs for more effective disaster response. The time Michael spent in training and educating has provided a great clarity of what works and what doesn't in the global efforts to bring about a new paradigm for those who are impoverished and those who seek to resolve its often perpetual nature.

Richard Lackey: What was the problem you were trying to solve?

Michael McCausland: Globally, we are experiencing a growing crisis of dependency stemming from the currently accepted belief that giving people things for free helps to create sustainable solutions. Most humanitarian missions, and even corporate social responsibility projects create dependency by giving people free things. Dependency stifles creativity, robs people of their dignity, discourages ownership and personal responsibility, and does not create sustainable solutions. Our model is to empower local leaders with self-sustainable solutions through local asset based development. We change their thinking about sustainability so they take new actions. We help build local capacity to break dependency on outside resources.

RL: What were some of the influences to your business model?

MM: Our approach to sustainability has been influenced by talking with successful practitioners from all over the world. We call our model – crowd sourced and experientially based. We have been inspired by local practitioners that have been thinking outside the box. They were not limited by what they currently had, but through creativity, innovation, ownership and personal responsibility, they were able to see new opportunities and create sustainable businesses for income generation and growth. They were also able to enhance community resiliency through the development of local private sector assets for disaster preparedness and response.

RL: What makes this business unique? Please use specifics.

MM: Our approach is unique in that we help local leaders use what they already have to build local capacity for self-sustainable solutions. We don't look for solutions through the provision of resources or solutions from outside the community. We start with an asset assessment to discover local resources. Then we work with local leaders to explore options for self-sustainable solutions designed to create resilient communities and sustainable income opportunities.

RL: What resources did you draw on for leadership and expertise?

MM: Leadership and expertise was gained through interaction with successful practitioners from around the world. What types of local asset-based development projects have been successful? What were the primary reasons for their success? Were there foundational principles that influenced their success and were those principles transferrable to other societies and communities? We felt that the answer to those questions was yes. We don't go in to new communities with solutions, but instead provide principles and practices for new ways of thinking that lead to new types of actions leading to local leaders solving local problems with local resources.

RL: What were some of the challenges in getting things done?

MM: The greatest challenge we have faced is the paradigm of dependency that has been created around the world, especially in locations where aid and support has already been provided. People have been conditioned to believe that they need help from the outside to solve their problems. They have been conditioned to rely on others to provide for their needs. They believe they are victims waiting to be rescued. When this mindset is established, people have a very difficult time shifting to a mindset of taking personal responsibility and ownership for solving their own problems and lifting themselves out of their current circumstances.

RL: Have you found synergy with other organizations, and if so, which?

MM: Yes, we have found synergy with other organizations, but they are few. Many organizations today use the term "sustainable" but they still give people free things. There are few organizations that truly understand the concept of local asset-based development. Most of the organizations that we are currently partnering with are either successful entrepreneurial oriented business professionals who understand the concept of building something from nothing or local practitioners that have already done what others said could not be done by creating local self-sustainable solutions without outside support or resources.

RL: What has been the most surprising thing to happen in your venture?

MM: The two things that have surprised me the most in our work are, 1) how tightly people hold on to their old paradigms and how much energy they will take to justify their way of doing things, even when it doesn't work or is not fruitful, and 2) how quickly people can change when they make the paradigm shift into self-sustainable solutions through local asset-based development.

RL: What is your vision for the future?

MM: Our vision is to continue to gather successful thought leaders and practitioners together to share, learn, grow, and propagate the model of self-sustainable solutions through local asset-based development. The more people that make the shift, the more people there are to share the concept. We must see exponential growth in order to address the growing global crisis of dependency.

RL: Is your operational structure different from a typical for-profit or not-for-profit business?

MM: Our operational structure is different in that we are always focusing on empowering local leaders instead of building our own infrastructure. We promote a decentralized model of operations. Each organization that we work with is autonomous and independent but they are bound by a common DNA and interconnected through a common road map and vehicle. The road map is provided by training programs that provide a common language and process and the vehicle for interaction is achieved through a common website. Two global viral growth networks have emerged from our work and they include the International Disaster Response Network and the Business Development Initiatives Network.

The International Disaster Response Network (www.IDRN.info) currently has over 10,000 photo identification badge members in almost 50 countries. The IDRN helps build community resiliency by organizing local private sector based capacity for disaster preparedness and response. Working together, IDRN members have moved over 200+ million dollars in goods and services in response to disaster situations.

The Business Development Initiatives Network (www.BDIN.org) has launched over 2,000 new businesses in 20+ countries with 73% sustainability. That means that 73% of all businesses ever started are still in operation.

RL: How do you market your business? What are your best tools?

MM: Our operational expansion is based on friendship. The DNA of our network is "friends working with friends, having fun, and changing the world". When we work with friends and achieve success, those friends tell other friends, and the network grows. We don't work anywhere unless we are invited. When we are invited to help local leaders with new ways of thinking, it's because a friend has invited us to help.

RL: What do you feel is the gap in what we as a population are trying to accomplish regarding benevolence?

MM: The biggest problem is that we create dependency by trying to help people by giving them free things. The gap could be identified as a lack of understanding by most humanitarian and aid organizations, missions groups, and corporate social responsibility programs on what constitutes and enables truly sustainable development. The gap is one of knowledge and understanding that leads to enforcing the continued mindset of dependency.

RL: What advice would you give to someone starting a unique business like yours?

MM: Learn from others. Our goal is to help others find the solutions to their own problems. We don't have their solutions, they do. We need to help them learn what those solutions are. Don't give people the solution. Those who provide the solution, own the solution. People only commit to what they help create. Local ownership is enhanced by local solutions.

RL: What kind of books do you read? What resources do you use for research? News?

MM: There are some good books about the dependency problem like:
Dead Aid by Dambisa Moyo
When Helping Hurts by Steve Corbett and Brian Fikkert.

I also like books about decentralized and viral growth networks and would recommend books like:
True Believer; Thoughts on the Nature of Mass Movements by Eric Hoffer
Starfish and the Spider by Ori Brafman and Rod Beckstrom
Tribes by Seth Godin
The World is Flat by Thomas Friedman

But a lot of our resources, news, and innovative ideas come from emerging thought leaders and practitioners on the front lines that are proving the concepts on a daily basis.

RL: How did your background or life events play into this venture?

MM: We started a humanitarian organization called Humanitarian International Services Group (www.HISG.org) the day before 9/11 on 9/10/01. After 13 years in the field, 130 countries, and millions of dollars invested, we learned all the things that didn't work. Like Thomas Edison said, we learned 1,000 ways not to make a light bulb. The most significant thing we learned was about how aid creates dependency and stifles growth and self-sustainability. The lesson was so significant we changed our name, narrowed our focus, and improved our principle-based models. Our new organization, Sustainable Communities Worldwide (www.SCWorldwide.org) is on a mission to empower local leaders with self-sustainable solutions through local asset-based development.

RL: What role do you feel the free markets and for-profit businesses will play going forward in solving the world's most dire problems?

MM: I think that true business is the cornerstone of a functioning society. As people use their individual gifts and talents to serve others, they receive a payment in return and we call this work or business. When people employ their gifts and talents through the establishment of a local company they can create a local self-sustainable income generation solution. When the economy of a local society is designed around local production and local consumption, the community can become self-sustainable.

Tyler Hartung: The Unreasonable Institute

Tyler Hartung is the co-founder and COO of Unreasonable Institute, a non-profit organization based in Boulder, Colorado that gives an "unreasonable advantage" to entrepreneurs who are creating solutions to the world's biggest social and environmental problems. The Institute does this by bringing entrepreneurs together to live under the same roof for five weeks, where they connect with mentors, investors, and a lasting global network of support. The Institute's goal is to help each of these ventures scale up to meaningfully impact the lives of over one million people.

Richard Lackey: What was the problem that you saw in the marketplace that you were trying to solve with the founding of the Unreasonable Institute?

Tyler Hartung: The problem was very close to home. All of the founders of the Institute were in some way seeking to be entrepreneurs in the social/environmental space. We said, "It would be great to start a company and use entrepreneurship to tackle problems." So then each of us on our own said, "Well, where do we go? Where are the resources for that? Whom do I talk to? Who can fund this? I'm twenty-something and I have no idea where to go to get help." And that was the need we each saw in our own respective ways.

We each thought, "Are there organizations out there that are successfully supporting entrepreneurs?" The answer was absolutely "yes"—in the tech space. There's Y Combinator, and it's specifically for tech startups, which is right here in our backyard. They're supporting and launching companies with great efficiency in the tech space, and we thought, "Wow, this is amazing. Is there anything like that for social and environmental entrepreneurs?"

And the answer was "no." We didn't find anything. There's a conference here and a university program there. But there was nothing as comprehensive as what we were looking for—a full-fledged suite of support for entrepreneurs tackling social and environmental problems. Since we didn't see it out there but yet we saw a model that was working in the tech space, we decided to adapt that model and bring it to social and environmental entrepreneurs.

RL: What were some of your influences? You talked about tech, but were there other influences to your business model outside of tech?

TH: The industry allowed us to come in with a very open mind and to focus not on what had been done historically but what worked right now. We took inspiration from people like Paul Pollack, who's been a recent student mentor and who's helped over twenty million farmers to come out of poverty. He had done that by *not* giving them something for free. He charged them for it. So the fact that we charge our entrepreneurs who come to our program was definitely not being done in the social and environmental space. But we did that because we believed that people are committed when they have to pay for something. That was really an inspiration.

RL: That's using a free market model for what you're doing. What was the response for the charge given the fact that you focus on development and socially responsible initiatives? What was the response for charging for that?

TH: We had three hundred applicants from over forty countries, and we got an amazing first class. I think there were probably some people who were questioning it, but we got exactly what we were looking for in great numbers; we even had to turn some people away who we thought were great applicants. And so even in that first year, before we'd ever done anything, I think the value that we were offering was very clearly greater than the cost. The first class came together nicely and people—including the mentors—said, "Because you have this charge in place, entrepreneurs are really brought into the program."

Now the other thing is we didn't let the entrepreneurs themselves pay the tuition cost in the first year. They literally were not allowed to pay it on their own. We made them go out and raise it from the crowd, if you will, from their communities. And so we had a funding platform where they reached out to their networks and would raise their tuition dollars.

RL: Did you find that the crowd-funded tuition payment then gave them an existing network in which to launch the business, or did that not translate?

TH: For the people who already had a large social network, it definitely allowed them to expand and to engage that social network in a meaningful way, in the sense that they weren't just saying, "Hey here's an update on what we're doing." They were saying, "Hey guys, here's a program that we think would be extremely valuable and we could leverage it in building the business. We need your help to get to it." That was for those who already had a good social network. Now for those who didn't, maybe they were from developing countries where access to the internet and the use of social networks and crowd funding is not very common. While they were still able to gain support, it was much harder for them to meet their funding goals. But they were able to gain notoriety as well as financial support from hundreds of people around the world with whom they would have never come into contact with if it were not for this marketplace. And so I think there were varying levels of growth beyond what their social network already was. I think everyone benefited in some way from this project.

RL: I know that you have a unique business model, but can you give us some specific examples of what is unique about the Unreasonable Institute as compared to Y Combinator or other business development groups?

TH: The first thing, again, is that while we charge our entrepreneurs, we don't take equity. We're taking both for-profit and non-profit companies. You can't take equity in a non-profit. I don't think the companies that we're supporting have the potential for launch, financial growth, and then exit, like they do in the tech space. And so equity again doesn't make sense.

In addition, we don't want to become biased towards those high growth companies. We want to be biased towards impact. And so if our focus were on equity, then you know we would inherently need to turn down a company that could have greater impact but would see lower financial returns to pay for the one that has higher financial returns but potential lower impact.

I think the other important and interesting aspect of our business model is that we run it fairly lean. In those first years our team needed three full-time people and then it kind of went up to four, and it's been hovering right around five people for all the things that we do now which includes growing our own Institute, supporting eight Institutes, ventures that have come through, helping them connect with funders and raising over thirty million dollars, and now launching two new Institutes. We do that all with a team of about five people.

RL: Wow.

TH: And with a small budget. Our budget is less than a million dollars a year. I think that's the interesting thing. Our business model is not too crazy beyond that. We receive grants and donations, and we also rely on people who volunteer their free time. Our mentors all come to the Institute and we don't have to pay them anything. They're one of the most valuable aspects of the Institute and they donate their time to us. That allows us to add a ton of value without having a high overhead.

RL: What resources do you draw on, or did you draw on, for leadership and experience, both for the Institute and your fellows?

TH: We came in knowing what we wanted to do, but we were really open and honest with people that we didn't necessarily know how to get there. And that we didn't have all the right answers.

A lot of time people who are starting up companies say, "Oh, you know, here's the right thing to do and here's what we're going to do." And you come out with confidence, whether it's real confidence or just a false front.

But we went to conferences and we had conversations with people and said, "We know what we want to do. We know the type of entrepreneur we want to support, but we need your help and advice." We saw someone who could be a potential mentor, potential funder, potential entrepreneur that we're developing a program for, and we said, "How would you foresee this playing out? What things would be more valuable or less valuable?" And we were doing that in the early days, as well as continuing that humility of not really knowing the right answer, not pretending that we knew all the answers throughout our programs. That really helped us attract many of the mentors. They felt that they truly were involved in the creation process.

Even during our six-week institute we ask entrepreneurs, funders, and mentors for feedback in modifying the program. I think it really helps to bring a lot of resources in. These are people who have a mission that they believe in, but they need my help. And so I'm excited about that as opposed to just trying to advise and mentor someone who has all the answers.

RL: How did your personal background or life events play into you getting involved with the Unreasonable Institute?

TH: There was no "ah-ha" moment. I think it was growing up and having something like empathy instilled within me, to care for others, and to think of how others are feeling. And I think it was realizing that, you know what? All the things that I had—education, access to university, access to jobs that pay me well, and a life free of stress—weren't things that I had to work for. They were things that were really inherent to where I was and the situation that I was born into. And at the same time, people are born into situations where no matter how hard they work those opportunities are not there. Those people are limited by their circumstances. And I'm fortunate due to my circumstances.

RL: What are some of the challenges you've found in getting things done?

TH: I think that being an accelerator program we are in the middle of ecosystems of people—entrepreneurs, other accelerators, service providers, funders, and mentors. And so we can get quite easily pulled in a lot of directions. I think the hardest thing is to identify what is the most important thing right now; like to put other opportunities on hold and to say "no." Because when an entrepreneur emails you asking for help and support, you want to say "yes." In those early days when we weren't as busy, we'd try and give them time, and read through their business plan and maybe give them some feedback. But even today, I get people emailing me saying, "I'd love your feedback on what I'm doing. I'd love to have an hour, or a half-hour phone call with you to discuss my business plan."

I just say, "You know I wish I could, but we have eighty-two entrepreneurs whom we're already supporting and more whom we're *trying* to support." So regretfully I must say "no" to them.

RL: Have you have found synergy with any other organizations?

TH: Yes, absolutely. If you go on to our website, we have a partners page that has over two hundred partner organizations. These are other organizations that support entrepreneurs.

They're university programs, other accelerators, and conferences. And these are what we call our pipeline partners who have the same goals as we do. Let's help these entrepreneurs who are tackling social and environmental problems, and move their businesses forward significantly. It's a lot of working together to help entrepreneurs navigate the network of support that exists for them. Our pipeline partners are essential to us finding entrepreneurs in over sixty countries, and for us to support those entrepreneurs when they go back to those countries.

The other is, of course, the funders. We have many funders who are looking to do deals themselves, whether it be to donate to companies or to invest in companies. But there are many funders who, just like our mentors, have hung out in the Institute and have spent a few days there, even without the ability to fund our entrepreneurs. Maybe let's say they focus on a really specific industry and none of the entrepreneurs are working on that. Well, these people will still come out to the Institute with the goal of helping our entrepreneurs better understand the investment process, be better prepared for it, and start asking the right questions that will help our entrepreneurs succeed. And they do sit down with the right mentors. So again, those are people who are just giving their time to support these entrepreneurs even if there's nothing other than maybe some inspiration and the feeling of helping that that person will get out of it.

RL: What has been the most surprising thing to happen as you guys have launched the Unreasonable Institute?

TH: I never expected the community to come together in such a powerful way that would last for so long. What I mean by that is that I expected people to come together for ten weeks. Then it was six weeks, now it's down to five. And for those multiple weeks, they'd have a nice, good time and take a lot of value from it, but then go back and just focus on their venture.

But there's an additional thing, which is the creation of a really powerful network that has lasted the test of time. It's a growing network between not just the entrepreneurs but between the other pipeline partners, the funders who came out, and, of course, the mentors and staff that the entrepreneurs interacted with. I never expected that to be so strong and so robust and to last so long.

RL: What do you guys actually consider yourself? A business development group or a business accelerator?

TH: An accelerator. I like that and I don't like it, because "accelerator" seems finite, and our job and our goal is to create a network of support for entrepreneurs that can last forever. I know it sounds a bit glossy, but really, if you're creating a network of people who can come together and support each other, that network might include entrepreneurs, mentors, funders, and corporations. It can last forever. I feel it's to a point at Unreasonable where for an organization to exist the network and the connectedness of the network would continue forever. And so we're an accelerator, but the only reason I don't like that word is it seems finite. You know you can't accelerate forever, but that's kind of what we're trying to do.

RL: And then because you're a little bit different than everyone else, is your management team structure different than the typical either for-profit business or accelerator? Are you a top-down, or more of a flat company?

TH: We're definitely a collaborative company. We're a mission-driven and values-driven company. So we focus on whether we're achieving our mission, which is to give a long-term unreasonable advantage to entrepreneurs and their ventures that are tackling the world's greatest challenges.

We ask ourselves difficult questions. Are we doing our job in a way that aligns with our values? Are we treating people like we're some sort of messiah? Are we humble? Are we feeling really transparent, and are we leading with truthfulness? Are we leading into fear? Are we stepping into fear and trying to be courageous in the things that we're doing? Are we being agile and always experimenting? Are we doing what works? Are we getting stuff done and are we remembering to dance along the way? These problems will still exist when we die, so if we wait till they're fully solved then we'll never see the chance to dance along the way. So that's what I mean. That's kind of like what our team is driven around—mission and values.

RL: What are some other interesting approaches to benevolent companies or socially responsible for-profit companies that you've seen?

TH: There's an interesting variety. Things like shifting mainstream finance into funding some of our biggest problems. Take solar. There's a company called Mosaic. They make it, so they're decreasing the cost. One of the biggest costs of solar energy in the United States, at least what I hear, is in the financing cost. They are decreasing the financing cost by allowing accredited investors in communities to fund solar projects. And those investors will then earn a return on that. So they're making something that can eventually move to the mainstream financial markets and completely revolutionize solar funding and the amount of funding going to solar projects.

Another example in the United States is Rework. I think one of the biggest needs in the space is actually talent, and young grads or people looking to change careers who need to find a job in the space and one that fulfills that. That's what Rework is tackling. They're helping people find meaningful work. They're more or less like a headhunter-slash-job placement company for people that they screen through their process. The look for people who are looking to do something good in the world, and they're helping facilitate that.

There are many interesting companies that we have been working with in Africa, for example, that are taking what are generally discarded things and turning them back into useful things. Waste Enterprises in Ghana operates in a place where, normally, human feces is dumped straight into the ocean, right in the main city. And they take that, and instead of having it being dumped into the ocean, they work with people who will pay them to take it. So people collecting human waste will actually pay Waste Enterprises to take it, and Waste Enterprises turns it into fuel and then sells it to places in Europe, to the EU where they have renewable energy standards and they can burn this converted human waste in coal plants.

RL: What is your vision for the future for the Unreasonable Institute?

TH: Our vision is to both deepen the value that we're adding to entrepreneurs and expand the breadth of entrepreneurs that we're supporting. We do think that value means to not be looking at our support of them as like, "What can we help with in the five weeks or the one year that they're actually an Unreasonable fellow?" We say, "What does it take to actually help this entrepreneur go from where they are to a company that is helping a million people?" And then to help them keep going beyond that.

So that means a lot of things outside of the five-week program. Building many more ongoing parts—service provider, partnerships, and lasting mentorships. Things like executive coaching for the entrepreneurs. Always be connecting them to new funders. That's like what it is for a single entrepreneur to deepen the level of support.

We want to help more entrepreneurs. At the Boulder Institute we're helping twelve ventures or so per year, so that's about twenty-five entrepreneurs per year. With those numbers we're going to do little to dent the course of history and turn it in our favor. So we've gone beyond that. Now we're launching an Institute in East Africa and an Institute in Mexico that are run by local teams; highly entrepreneurial teams that have done a lot of good work in the past. And those guys are going to be supporting a whole new cohort of entrepreneurs in those locations. The network that we have built at the Unreasonable Institute in Boulder can help a new one form in East Africa, a new one form in Mexico, and now these three networks can work together. And then we'll be launching new Institutes beyond that. So our ultimate goal is to have one hundred Institutes in one hundred countries.

I think that beyond new locations there will be a focus on issue areas, like a focus on technology for example. We could say we're going to run an Unreasonable Institute that's focused on entrepreneurs who are dealing with issues in the ocean. Or we could say we're going to do an Unreasonable Institute for entrepreneurs who are strong in distribution in East Africa. And you can, by focusing in those ways, bring in the most world class mentors, corporate partners, funders, and service providers that are really hyper-focused on those issues, on those technologies, or on those kinds of areas that are important to you. So that's kind of where we're going in the coming years.

RL: What advice would you give to someone starting a socially responsible or benevolent company? I have heard you say a quote about dancing along the way. It always stuck with me.

TH: If you're going to start a company you're going to have to be in it for the long haul. And it's even harder if you're tackling social or environmental problems. The problem that you're going to tackle is probably still going to exist when you die. And so if you're waiting to completely eradicate that problem you're never going to have one hundred percent success. The quote that I gave was from Emma Goldman, who said, "I don't want to be a part of your revolution if I can't dance along the way." And so basically the point there is like, hey, you have to celebrate the small victories as you're building your company. Celebrate the first life, and in fact celebrate the one hundredth or two hundredth. Celebrate moving to a new location. Celebrate hiring your fifth employee. Celebrate things like that along the way, or else you're going to burn out. So that would be the advice I'd give.

RL: What role do you feel that the free markets and for profit businesses will play going forward in solving the world's greatest and most dire problems?

TH: To me, business is the most ubiquitous, wide-reaching and impactful mechanism in the world. It touches most people's lives.

The most important work in the world is the work of the social and environmental entrepreneurs. If you want to improve those lives you need to improve business, and that's what these entrepreneurs are doing. Our job is simply to do whatever we can to support them. We're there to bring resources to them. We're there to be in the background, because they're the true rock stars. They're the ones putting it on the line. They're the ones operating where the rubber meets the road and the impact actually takes place. So if I can say that in the course of my life I helped these entrepreneurs and those entrepreneurs went on doing these things, I can die happy.

Hendrik Jordaan: One Thousand & One Voices

Long deprived of patient foreign capital, Africa is now seeing an influx of private equity funds. In May 2013, John K. Coors announced that together with more than ten other wealthy families he was setting up a private equity fund to invest $300 million within Africa, with up to $100 million by the end of that year to invest in the fastest-growing African nations including Kenya, Ghana, Tanzania, and Nigeria. The fund would invest over the next four years while recruiting more families to contribute. "What allows businesses to create jobs and grow is investment capital, and patient capital is what the continent needs right now," Coors said. The group is willing to stay invested for a decade or longer, and to share the expertise of the group's wealthy investors. Hendrik Jordaan, a former attorney at Morrison & Foerster LLP, serves as the group's chief executive.

Richard Lackey: What's your strategy for improving the quality of life in the areas you've targeted?

Hendrik Jordaan: Neither philanthropy nor short-term private equity is the solution to create jobs to lift people out of poverty. The role of job creation, which is what we're focused on, is the world of free enterprise done well.

My theory of change, very simply put, is that to lift people out of poverty and to generate prosperity, people need jobs. They need jobs that they can be proud of. To have jobs, you need profitable companies. And companies that are profitable need capital. But they don't only need cash. And that's where traditional private equity falls short. They need what we call three-dimensional capital.

The construct is that the world's leading families are in a unique place of opportunity and occupy a unique place of responsibility. That means that unlike traditional investors who must invest for the short term because their jobs depend on it or their monthly paycheck depends on it, the world's wealthiest families can be as patient as they need to be. It's patient financial capital, not a ten-year fund. Performance is twenty-years plus. It's a longer investment period and a unique fund structure that's designed around patience.

We call it legacy investment. You're building for your name but not for your numbers.

As we model our deals on a perspective of the return on investment, from an ROI perspective we intend to outperform all of the major firms over the long run. We're not about short term. We're not about chasing short-term yield, but long term.

From a pure portfolio management perspective, what appeals to families is capital preservation. For the world's wealthiest families, that's more important than return.

RL: Is that because they don't need more money? They want to preserve what they have.

HJ: Right. So when you can be long term, you're actually lower risk. You're after high ROI. So three-dimensional capital is intellectual capital. That means we tap the business and intellectual acumen of the John Coors family. With relational capital it's leveraging. One of the family members, for instance, is leveraging their net worth to help add value to one of the portfolio companies.

And we can be looking, for instance, at building out of distribution. If they have relationships and contacts around the globe they can add that element of capital to the equation. You know they're bringing not only their money that can stay awhile but they're bringing relationships around the globe. They're bringing intellectual capital, which is, like, "Hey, I used to be the CEO of a brewing company." This CEO can get on the phone with the CEO of a brewing company in Africa to talk through a strategic issue.

The way we think of it is we're not an impact fund. We're the world's leading families investing with impact.

When we talk about traditional fund management you've got an income side and growth side and all the others. But inside the growth parameters there are several pieces.

RL: Would you compare this to deep value investing? Is growth revenue based or is there an expected social impact?

HJ: The upside is absolutely evident. When these businesses grow, the dynamics of the entire community can change for the better.

RL: So, how exactly is the risk managed for each venture?

HJ: You mitigate risk through the deployment of three-dimensional capital. Let's just take a family office. They could look at us in a variety of ways because we're not pigeonholed. Could we be considered somebody's private equity Africa exposure? Of course. But it could also be considered a different market as well. So I think it just depends on the advisor, the consultant who you know is working with a family themselves. They may want to look at this as something that they're directly involved in and they don't want to bring in their advisor to get his two cents.

RL: So they're actively involved in this.

HJ: Yes, they're actively involved. So it might fall outside of the realm of their overall strategic asset allocation.

RL: Okay. So what's the third piece to that?

HJ: It's intellectual, relational, and patient financial. Talking about de-risking deals, when you first know in terms of macro investment the development thesis-let's say we're looking at a mining services job-when you have the world's two or three leading mining families, they'll look at the deal and say, "You know we've done this for seventy-plus years and we tell you this is what we see and this is what we think. Oh, and by the way, we're investing the deal and we're investing alongside it." Okay? That's like ten times the credibility of even the largest funds or money management firms.

So point one, your theory of identification. Point two, you need diligence. I called up mining family X. They got their CEO to look at the portfolio company, spent a day, boom, cut through it. Right? So we're already seeing that. Point three, operational value adds de-risk. So you take things such as execution risk, which is a big issue in Africa.

RL: Could you give an example?

HJ: Let's say you invest in Nigeria and you're investing alongside one of the leading families in Nigeria. You know you've got access to their talents. They could parachute the talent in. You've got less corruption risk and you've got less risk overall. And so it's just a slew of issues that go away when you partner with them.

RL: What's the greatest unforeseen risk in Africa?

HJ: Let's take an example. You look at a food services deal. You should have other contracts ready the day you close your deal to offset much of the risk by bringing in other parties that may need that food supply. Day one, you do research reduction. So that's the core of everything. I think the portfolio companies will look at what we can bring to the table. They're going to want you as a partner. We're bringing the most influential families from around the world. That can really add value.

RL: Absolutely. You become a preferred partner on multiple sides. So where does the values piece fit?

HJ: While we welcome investors from multiple regions and multiple religions around the world, each family in our movement passes a value screen.

RL: So share a little about how you bring people from such diverse backgrounds into what is becoming a global movement?

HJ: It's very important for us to have a truly global movement. Let me back up. One of the elements in having John Coors as a family is that everybody says, "What you have is an American who's been traditionally associated with conservative politics and is a well-known Christian. So put that in a small little box. That's what you're about." So the rest of the world is excluded? No. That's not what we're about, and the Coors family agrees. This is a movement that has certain immutable values, which has, as I mentioned, a couple of ways you can look at it. You can say the constructs of natural law. When you think of natural law, I think actually it winds up very well with the way Jesus lived his life. Its global principles.

Now I don't care if you're a self-proclaimed Christian or a self-proclaimed Hindu. You know that if your track record as a family is one that doesn't treat your neighbor like yourself and has demonstrated inconsistency with those values, then you're not welcome. Because that's not what we're about. That's not the family that we're building this on. We're building this on the principle of natural law, like the principles that Jesus lived his life on. Those are the values. And so what do they mean? That means risk taking. That means appropriate risk taking. I'll submit to you that it doesn't mean that you sit on your talents or your money or your gifts. No you do not.

RL: You leverage them.

HJ: You leverage and you work hard. It means you strive for excellence. It means you treat people the right way. It means that you're demanding in terms of how you operate your businesses. You're fair but you demand a lot. And that's how we operate our portfolio.

RL: Building free market solutions isn't easy, but you and the team at One Thousand & One Voices certainly do have a unique approach that should significantly enhance outcomes. Do you see Africa as fertile ground for free market solutions?

HJ: Incredibly fertile ground. In more than a dozen countries on the continent people are starting to see the benefits that free market solutions bring. It is always hard to change things, to give power back to the people, once governments control so much, but there are so many intelligent people desperate for change who have a heart and a passion to do well for their families and their country that they are quick to adapt when they see the benefits of free market solutions.

Steve Brooks: OZ Architecture

The Republic of Rwanda and City of Kigali commissioned OZ Architecture, based in Denver, Colorado, to create a conceptual master plan supporting Rwanda's vision to become an important center of stability and development for the continent of Africa. The vision has drawn global community interest, and the population of the capital city is growing rapidly. One focus was to create an urban center that accommodates anticipated growth and economic activity. A new city center incorporates sustainable housing, livable community concepts, renewable energy sources, green design, and a methodology for improving conditions in the informal hillside housing settlements, which captures the spirit of the new Rwandan society. The principal in charge of the project is Steve Brooks.

Richard Lackey: What was the problem OZ Architecture was trying to solve with the Kigali project?

Steve Brooks: We were asked by the government of Rwanda to do a master plan that supported the President's Vision 20/20 for Rwanda. We met with the president and said to him, "Why don't you do physical planning to give some flesh to your economic and government's plan?" When he agreed with that, we managed to get a contract started. But that's what we were after—giving a physical plan to support the Vision 20/20. We knew the problem to be solved wasn't really physical. But if you can get a linear physical process in front of people, then you can rally support, get people together, network, and build institutions. All kinds of things can come as a result of that.

RL: What were some of the influences on the business model being a public-private partnership? You were getting a contract from the government, so what were the influences on that?

SB: Let's talk about the nature of planning. What we try to do with planning is to create value, in that economic drivers are really what it's about. And that was something that we actually had to kind of backpedal on, because their expectation was that we come up with this master plan in the city, build it, and they would come. But we said, "No, this is going to be driven by the private sector. You're going to have developers and investors come here and say, 'I want to build a building' or 'I want to do a development because...'" And so you're creating a platform for that to happen. And you create value when you say, "This is a good location for a high density urban center." And then you get developers come in and identify that and they participate because of the idea.

RL: What resources did you draw on for leadership and expertise over there? You mentioned a business community. Was it strictly them, or other resources as well?

SB: We had a very participatory process. We met with the President. We met with ministers. We met with the Planning Department. We met with Mayors. And then we got out into the villages and talked with people. We got input from all sides. Some of it had to be a little bit under the radar because it was unofficial, such as going into the informal housing settlements and talking with people there. "How is it? What's it like to live here? What are your concerns? What are the biggest issues that you would like to see changed in the environment you're living in?" That kind of thing.

RL: What were some of the challenges?

SB: I would say the biggest challenge was not involvement or even defining the solutions, which was really a journey on its own. We didn't come there to bring our Western solutions or bring the Denver Tech Center to Rwanda, but to come up with uniquely Rwandan solutions to Rwandan problems. So the problem wasn't really on that end. The biggest challenge was the capacity on the implementation end, which is something we're still struggling with a bit. Did we get the message across? Did the master plan ideas get rooted so that they would survive and they would create a sustainable situation moving forward?

RL: Have you found synergies with other organizations throughout this process? How did you incorporate non-profits into the mix?

SB: Yes. First of all, we had a large team of consultants that were part of it. We had environmental engineers, civil engineers and landscape architects. We also invited Engineers without Borders and Water for People in because we saw that there would be some synergy even with non-profits to be involved because they had good ideas about how to do development and that kind of thing. Within the country we were getting ministries together for the first time. We got the Ministry for Infrastructure to talk with the city planners, and we started getting people to talk to each other, which was one of the things that we were kind of a catalyst for. It was institution building, because the people hadn't gotten together before. But when you have a project as big as a master plan for a capital city, you get a lot of people involved and you get all the diverse viewpoints in together.

RL: What was the most surprising thing to happen during the project?

SB: We were surprised by the seriousness with which people came to task. They were very serious and studious, and were really interested in taking the ideas forward and seeing a bright future. That was something that we started out with—how impressed we were with that. And how young the population was and how young some of these leaders were, because it's a young population. And how these young people have been given some big responsibilities and were taking them on with a lot of energy and seriousness. That was the first thing—how impressed we were with the people whom we were working with and their diligence and desire to do things.

And then we saw the national community come together. When I first went in 2004 there were over a hundred thousand people in prison for participating in the genocide. Now it's half that. Many of the people in prison were allowed to leave prison and go back to their communities if they confessed to what they did and took whatever restitution the community gave to them. And the result of that has been phenomenal. There has been reconciliation between the ethnic groups. There's been forgiveness among the individuals who were actually involved and who had family members killed. There's been forgiving of the person that did it. And when that happened the walls broke down—the walls of fear—and you can just imagine what it would be like to let this prisoner out who had killed your family. You know what it's going to be like to have them back in the community. But what really surprised us was how well that process worked. It's called "*gacaca*," which means "out on the lawn." They resolve these cases on the lawn—that is to say, outside of the formal courthouse system—and they get it settled and then they move forward and they don't go back.

RL: They never bring it up again?

SB: They move forward. They say, "We've got to get past this and this is the way we're going to do it and we're going to move on." And then when there's that kind of reconciliation the community comes together and they work together and it's amazing what happens.

RL: How did your background and life experiences play into this?

SB: I had lived in Uganda in 1992 and taught architecture at Makerere University, and found some students from Makerere there in Rwanda. So I had a passion and a certain understanding of East Africa from that experience. When the opportunity came to hook up with the president and get something rolling, I was on board and I was ready to do that. I wanted to get back to Africa after so many years.

RL: So what does the future hold? How is Rwanda going to get to the next level?

SB: It is a combination of government supporting business growth through thoughtful infrastructure development and nurturing the spirit of entrepreneurship by recruiting expertise in medicine, education, and all forms of business. But most importantly, the experts need to come in with a plan to serve and not to dictate.

Carole Canale: Rwanda Village Makeover

Carole Canale is president and founding director of Rwanda Village Makeover. Based in Denver, Colorado, the mission of the organization is: "To assist people in a way that creates self-reliance and impacts the quality of everyday life. To listen to the people and then originate projects and/or bring expertise to existing ones that work within the people's capacity to manage them and replicate them."

Richard Lackey: What was the initial problem you were trying to solve?

Carole Canale: For me personally, it was giving the people the opportunity to see their own abilities. There were definitely all kinds of need there. As is throughout most of Africa, you can go into almost any area and find need. But for me, I saw the people who didn't want a handout. I saw people who believed in themselves, but they definitely needed training and they were under-resourced. For me, the projects are an end result. It's really about the people, about empowering them and transferring skills and capacity to them. For them to be able to really use all their natural gifts.

RL: So when you got there, did you know a lot about Rwanda? Did you end up in one village or were you going there with this purpose? How did you get there?

CC: I had met Willy Rumenera, who's my on-ground partner over there in Rwanda. He introduced me to Steve (Brooks), and we just dreamed. We did one conference here. I think we had about thirty people show up and we just kind of laughed. And then the next year Steve joined us, and we had many more people there and some others engaged with it. Then Willy went back and we continued to talk about what we wanted to do, what was our purpose, and why we were put together like we were put together.

I went to Rwanda in 2007. We met with many of the national leaders including the mayor of Kigali and minister of Huye, the minister of education, different people in that realm, and they basically all said "Go to the village." So Willy spent the next year identifying with the village. Cyanika was one that we really felt drawn to. We were looking for certain things. We were looking for people who would engage at every level, and be able to manage projects once we left, and then also be able to replicate them.

RL: Can you talk a little bit about your business model and then also the influences that are on that business model? Whether it's personal or cultural or maybe a combination of both?

CC: I think it's really about empowering the people. I mean that's where my main focus is—the people. Going in and empowering them. For example, our *Each One Teach One* model. What we knew is the government had given the villagers rabbits, and the villagers had simply eaten the rabbits. In the absence of better information, this was a perfectly rational choice. We asked ourselves, could we have gone in and taught all the widows about the rabbits and how to manage them and envision them for a bigger picture? We knew we had to give them a bigger vision. We had to really help them to see what they could do with this.

We could have gone totally hands-on, but that wasn't what was going to create community.

When we got there we found ten churches, and the ten weren't speaking to each other. I mean not because they were angry with each other; they didn't share ideas. They were holding everything close to their vests.

We saw a lot of that within that community and so we wanted to build on that. We wanted to build that community and have them think of each other as neighbors, to help each other and share resources. And the Each One Teach One model was one way to do that.

We asked Willy to identify the head honcho. I asked him to please go find me the head widow. And he did. We asked her to put a small group together who would follow her lead and whom she was able to influence. We went in and we taught them and we commissioned them to train ten women after themselves.

The idea was for them to breed their rabbits and distribute the rabbits. That was their job. They had to keep teaching beyond themselves, and in a short period of time we had almost every widow involved. In fact we went beyond the widows into the desperately poor households, with women being trained and having the knowledge. Now they're not all doing the rabbit project, but they're trained in doing it. So they may be doing it a little bit at home. They're not doing it in the co-ops.

RL: Please walk me through the co-ops and how women are breeding generations of rabbits to sell at market.

CC: They sell them at a local market and to each other. A household that doesn't have rabbits might buy them. They're selling to restaurants too, but the hard part with the restaurant market is that we need to get rabbit carriers, because the women can't just carry these rabbits under their arms on the buses. At first, the rabbits rode on the buses. So we've got to build that market enough to be able to employ someone who will come and pick up the rabbits and take them to the restaurants. That's the next step.

RL: I know the first generation of rabbits was donated, but are they getting paid in rabbits? Are they being paid in currency? The co-op is a business, so what's its profit model?

CC: We call them cells. We have six cells now. The number of women in each cell varies from cell to cell. Those women divide up the rabbits equally. They keep all the money that comes in from the rabbits in one bank account. They require three signatures on it. I did not set that up. They set that up themselves. They pool the money for two to three months, and then they collectively decide what they're going to do with the money.

RL: And do they usually fund a project?

CC: They do in some cases. Sometimes they re-invest in their own projects, and other times they save to launch new projects.

RL: What other changes in the people or community have you seen as a result of the growing market?

CC: The last time I was there I saw the woman whom I call the Head Honcho—because I can't pronounce her name—and I did not recognize her. I asked Willy where she was. He said, "Carole, that's her." And I said, "But she looks so different." She was so vibrant and full of life, and she had gained weight. Her face was full, where before her appearance was gaunt. And I said, "She doesn't even look like herself." And he said, "Because of the rabbit project she's able to buy the HIV meds that she needs." Her whole countenance was different. She now had a vibrancy that wasn't there before. She had life in her that I didn't see before.

RL: You've mentioned several projects, but let's say starting with the rabbits or maybe the goats or the potatoes, are they all financially solvent? Are they running on their own now? What sort of challenges persist?

CC: Yes. As for the rabbit project, this is one thing I love about them. They share. I asked them, "How are things going? Tell me the good. Tell me the bad." They don't ask me, "Can you get us locks?", but they shared that they were having some theft problems because the locks were not secure enough. I went out and looked at them. In addition to poor or non-existent locks, the hinges were hardly functional. They were nailed in with crooked nails and hanging. You could put a screwdriver in there and just pop them out. Little things mean a lot here. The details are important.

The women also said that they were having a hard time knowing what was wrong with their rabbits, and the vets don't go out to the cells. And they don't have a way to carry the rabbits to the vet or to get there, and so it's this big guessing game. The women were really concerned about it. So I had my administrative assistant pull all 4-H materials on rabbits. She narrowed it down to a concise disease manual, and it's got pictures. The skin disease, the eye disease, the foot disease, whatever it is; it shows them visually and then gives them very simple guidance: "This is what it is. This is why it happened. This is how to prevent it."

RL: What is your vision for the project in the future?

CC: That the village will be self-supporting. That they're going to be okay. They're going to learn. They're going to have diverse diets. They're going to have enough money to live on. I'm not talking about making them rich.

I would like to see these people able to depend on themselves. I want them to be able to believe in themselves. And I think at the end of the day the community of Cyanika is not going to be known because of what they wanted or even because of what they accomplished. I think they're going to be known because of what they *believed*. They believed in themselves and they believed that they could do it.

RL: What drives this approach to helping people?

CC: Since I've been a young kid I've given everything away. I drove my father crazy. "You want my coat?" I'd say. "Here, take my coat." I have always had that drive in me to not have pity on anybody. I don't pity those people at all. They teach me things that I wish I had known earlier in life. You know that they're just amazing. So it's not about that and it's not about charity. I don't really get long-term charity efforts at all. I think charities can rob people of their dignity if they don't look to make the people they are helping sustainable over the long run. Unless it's an emergency situation like in Haiti, or an earthquake or a hurricane. That's different. That's not what I'm talking about. But if you want sustainability it's not charity.

RL: I completely agree with you. Where do you go for help to get help and unique ideas or solutions?

CC: For me, I welcome anybody, but I find tremendous resources at colleges and universities. I've worked at Stanford. I'm working with Duke. I'm working with CSU. I work with CU. I'm working with a gal out of Madison. I love young people because they have these really creative ideas that I don't have. And they have a whole lot more energy than I have. And they have book smarts. I love empowering young people to dream and to go after their dream and to do it.

RL: What advice would you give to someone who is starting a venture like yours?

CC: Invest in the people. Nobody wants to hear what you have to say until they know you *care*. If you don't know whether someone cares about you, are you going to listen to what they say? You'll get more mileage that way.

You can take a bunch of money and pour it in. We've watched it happen all around the world. And you know what? There was no investment in the people. There was no relationship there. Don't just give them what you want, take the time to find out what they need.

Chapter Five: Focus on Food

In previous chapters, we've taken a survey of many of the greatest challenges facing both impoverished peoples and those who have suffered from a natural disaster. The problems are both great and persistent: affordable energy, clean water, safe housing, education, health, freedom from civil strife, equal rights, and many more.

Hunger is a major challenge. On nearly every continent of the globe, millions of families face starvation and chronic malnutrition. Hunger has many causes, including long-term economic problems, drought, floods, human mismanagement, and environmental issues. This situation is even more heartbreaking because much of the world's food inequity is preventable. While many go hungry, millions of other families who live perhaps only a few hours away or across a national boundary—a line on a map—enjoy a life of plenty.

How long can a human being last without food? Dehydration—the lack of water—will kill you quickly; if completely deprived of water you can expect to be dead within three or four days. But food starvation is agonizing and slow. Generally, as long as victims are properly hydrated, experience has shown that humans can survive without any food for thirty or forty days. Death can occur after as long a period as sixty days. But these numbers can vary considerably with the physical condition of the victim; a victim suffering from the stresses of a post-disaster environment or a child in Sub-Saharan Africa who is already undernourished will die much more quickly.

While starvation is a serious global problem, sustained undernourishment and malnutrition are far more widespread, and the effects are perhaps even more damaging. According to the United Nations World Food Programme, in the world today an estimated 870 million people do not have enough to eat. While this number has improved since 1990, progress slowed after the Great Recession of 2008.

Sustained hunger kills more people than AIDS, malaria, and tuberculosis combined. The vast majority of chronically hungry people—ninety-eight percent—live in developing countries, where almost fifteen percent of the population is undernourished. The largest share of the world's hungry people (roughly 563 million) live in Asia and the Pacific. One in four of the world's children exhibit stunted growth. In developing countries the proportion can rise to one in three. One out of six children—roughly one hundred million—in developing countries is underweight.

While malnutrition can happen anywhere, particularly after a natural disaster, eighty percent of the world's stunted children live in just twenty countries. Sixty-six million primary school-age children across the developing world attend classes hungry, with twenty-three million in Africa alone. The World Food Programme calculates that $3.2 billion is needed per year to reach all sixty-six million hungry school-age children.

We can pinpoint the geographical areas of most intense malnutrition. The Global Hunger Index (GHI) was developed by the International Food Policy Research Institute (IFPRI), and was first published in 2006 with the Welthungerhilfe, a German non-profit organization (NGO). A year later the Irish NGO Concern Worldwide joined the group as co-publisher. The GHI is an annual multidimensional statistical tool used to describe the state of the hunger situation in the nations of the world. The Index ranks countries on a scale of one hundred points, with zero being the ideal score ("no hunger") and one hundred being the theoretical worst. The higher the score, the worse the food situation of a country.

The 2012 GHI was calculated for 120 developing countries and countries in transition, fifty-seven of which exhibited a serious or worse hunger situation. Across these developing countries, 14.7 was the average score. Many nations, both developed and emerging, post scores of five or below. In 2012, the People's Republic of China—the place where your parents told you was full of starving people—scored a very respectable 5.1, indicating that this highly populous nation has managed to cast off the failed policies of dictatorial collectivism that led to serious problems of malnutrition during the latter half of the twentieth century. In contrast, India, which is still saddled with tremendous government inefficiencies, posted a score of 22.9, which is shockingly high.

The worst score of 37.1 was given to Burundi, the landlocked country in East Africa bordered by Rwanda to the north, Tanzania to the east and south, and the Democratic Republic of the Congo to the west. One of the five poorest countries in the world, Burundi has one of the lowest per capita gross domestic products of any nation in the world. With a population of about ten million, since its independence in 1962 the country has suffered from political corruption, tribal warfare, poor access to education, and the effects of HIV/AIDS. Throughout the twentieth century, famines and food shortages occurred throughout Burundi.

106

According to the World Food Programme, 56.8% of children under age five suffer from chronic malnutrition. Not surprisingly, the average life expectancy in Burundi is fifty-three years, putting it near the bottom of the list. (The longest are Japan, Switzerland, and San Marino, where the average lifespan is eighty-three years.)

Burundi's story is not as sad as it is frustrating. Much like Haiti and dozens of other nations around the globe, if under a structure where government and free markets worked together, the abundance of natural resources that have been wastefully exploited would provide a much higher standard of living.

North Korea

No discussion of food insecurity that is directly caused by the actions of a central government would be complete without mentioning the twenty-first century's most bizarre and repressive regime, the ironically named Democratic People's Republic of Korea.

North Koreans are no strangers to famine. During the worst recent famine that lasted from 1994 to 1998, while an exact statistical number of deaths will probably never be fully determined, many experts estimate between 800,000 and 1.5 million people died due to starvation, disease, or sickness caused by lack of food. Higher estimates range from two to three million.

In 2011, during a visit to North Korea, former US President Jimmy Carter reported that one third of children in North Korea were malnourished and stunted in their growth because of a lack of food. He also said that the North Korean government had reduced each person's daily food intake from 1,400 calories to 700 calories. Presumably this reduction did not apply to members of the military and to residents of Pyongyang, who are always given resource priority.

In perhaps the cruelest of any government action in recent history, in April of 2012 thousands of people may have starved in the fertile North Korean grain-growing region at the same time the country was staging a mass celebration to commemorate the one-hundredth anniversary of the birth of the nation's founder, Kim Il-sung. Because of worsening food shortages, there were reports of people starving to death even in South and North Hwanghae provinces, the country's agricultural heartland. Good Friends, a Seoul-based aid group, said on its website that starvation claimed victims throughout South Hwanghae. At Hwanghae

Steelworks some workers had died because food rations stopped, it said. Six people—children or the elderly—died in just one village in Shingye county after the authorities released an emergency supply of only one or two kilograms (2.2 to 4.4 pounds) of corn to each household. Other sources reported that in April, ten people had died of starvation on each collective farm in and around the coastal city of Haeju following shortages in late winter.

North and South Hwanghae both saw rice production fall in 2012 due to flooding, and most of the autumn harvest was diverted to the military or for citizens of Pyongyang. In South Hwanghae shortages were aggravated by restrictions on market trading and travel during the one-hundred-day mourning period for leader Kim Jong-il, the son of, and successor to, Kim Il-sung, who died on December 17, 2011. One report published in April 2012 by the *Tokyo Shimbun*, a Japanese newspaper, claimed that since the death of Kim Jong-il, twenty thousand people had starved to death in South Hwanghae Province.

Meanwhile, just south of the Demilitarized Zone lies the Republic of Korea. An economic powerhouse, South Korea has a market economy which ranks fifteenth in the world by nominal GDP and is one of the G-20 major economies. It is a high-income developed country and the most industrialized member country of the Organization for Economic Co-operation and Development (OECD). South Korea is the only developed country so far to have been included in the group of Next Eleven countries. South Korea had one of the world's fastest-growing economies from the early 1960s to the late 1990s, and it is still one of the fastest-growing developed countries in the 2000s, along with Hong Kong, Singapore, and Taiwan, the other three Asian Tigers.

But South Korea is not Utopia. While it enjoys a booming industrial economy, South Korea must import ninety percent of its food. Food stability in South Korea has experienced a continuous decline, caused by rapidly increased grain price volatility and intensified import source concentration as the western countries, particularly the United States and the European Union, devote more and more of their corn production to biofuels. (It's estimated that thirty-five percent of corn production is now going into biofuels.) In addition, a report by Samsung Economic Research Institute entitled "New Food Strategies in the Age of Global Food Crises" said, "Food safety fell to its lowest level in 2008 at 94.2, down more than 5.85 compared to 2005, indicating a need for efforts to improve food safety, quality, soil, and ecosystems.....Once a food crisis occurs, excessive overseas dependence is greatly detrimental to food security, because it becomes very difficult to purchase food on international markets, regardless of the amount of foreign exchange reserves."

The Problem of Distribution

If someone—anyone—is going hungry or even starving anywhere in the world today, is the problem a lack of sufficient food being produced to satisfy the earth's growing population?

Not really. In a situation that's similar to the example of shoes in the previous chapter, there's enough food being produced—farm products, animal protein, and seafood—to provide for everyone on earth. According to the World Resources Institute, during the past several decades, global per capita food production has been increasing substantially. The term *dietary energy supply* is used to describe the food available for human consumption, usually expressed in kilocalories per person per day. It gives an overestimate of the total amount of food consumed as it reflects both food consumed and food wasted. It varies markedly between different regions and countries of the world.

According to the Food and Agriculture Organization of the United Nations, the average minimum daily energy requirement is about 1,800 kilocalories per person. The amount of food energy available and consumed by people of the world's nations varies considerably. Here are the top ten lowest and highest nations:

	Top Ten Nations	Daily dietary energy consumption per capita (2005-07)
1	United States	3,770
2	Austria	3,760
3	Greece	3,700
4	Luxembourg	3,690
5	Belgium	3,690
6	Italy	3,660
7	Malta	3,590
8	Portugal	3,580
9	France	3,550
10	Israel	3,540
	AVERAGE MINIMUM DAILY REQUIREMENT	**1,800**
	Bottom Ten Nations	
1	Democratic Republic of the Congo	1,590
2	Eritrea	1,590
3	Burundi	1,680
4	Haiti	1,850
5	Comoros	1,860
6	Zambia	1,890
7	Angola	1,950
8	Ethiopia	1,950
9	Central African Republic	1,960
10	Timor-Leste	2,020
Statistics from the Food and Agriculture Organization of the United Nations		

The fact is that when considered on a day-to-day basis, not even taking into consideration natural disasters such as floods and hurricanes, food distribution is highly uneven in many areas of the world. Some areas are chronically short while others enjoy abundance.

Regional Food Crises

Despite the robust production of food on a global scale, over the past fifty years the world has seen one food crisis after another. Many have occurred in Africa, which despite having rich resources is constantly battered by crises both natural and manmade. Indeed, countries such as the Democratic Republic of Congo and Nigeria are amongst the most resource-rich nations in Africa and should, based just on their natural resources, be amongst the wealthiest nations on the planet. Major African hunger crises include:

- Nigeria, 1967-1970: One million die in civil war and famine in the breakaway Biafran republic.
- Uganda, 1970s: Localized famine in Karamoja leaves thousands dead.
- Ethiopia, 1984-1985: Up to one million people die in famine caused by conflict, drought, and economic mismanagement.
- Somalia, 1991-1992: Drought and war contribute to famine across the country; about 250,000 famine-related deaths reported in 1992.
- Democratic Republic of Congo, 1998-2004: Severe food crisis caused by conflict, with millions affected by hunger.
- Ethiopia, 2000: Three consecutive years of drought leave millions at risk, with famine declared in Gode, the Somali region.
- Niger, 2005: Thousands die following drought and locust invasion.
- Sudan, 2008: Localized famine in some areas of southern Sudan due to war and drought.
- Niger, 2010: Food shortages affect more than seven million people after crops fail.
- Somalia, 2010-2012: Nearly 260,000 die of hunger caused by drought and conflict.

Vietnam

When shining a light on food insecurity, it would be too easy to report on the truly impoverished nations of the earth. The difficulties of undeveloped nations are extreme and well-known; many do not even have functioning economies.

A more useful example is the Socialist Republic of Vietnam. This Pacific Rim nation has come a long way from the ravages of the Vietnam War, and since 2000 its economic growth has been among the highest in the world. In 2011 it had the highest Global Growth Generators Index among eleven major economies. Its successful economic reforms resulted in it joining the World Trade Organization in 2007. On the United Nations' scale that measures daily dietary energy consumption per capita, a segment of which is reproduced earlier in this chapter, Vietnam is reported to provide 2,770 kilocalories per person per day, which puts it in the middle of the nations of the earth. Not the best, but certainly not the worst.

Due to its location, Vietnam is regularly pounded by typhoons that come roaring off the South China Sea. Every year, as many as thirteen tropical storms will reach the East Sea (which is what Vietnamese call the South China Sea), with half of them likely to hit Vietnam. Four of the ten storms that hit the East Sea in 2012 caused severe consequences to Vietnamese people and property, according to the National Steering Committee for Flood and Storm Prevention and Control.

One of the most destructive in recent times was Typhoon Son-Tihn, which in October 2012 moved along the Tonkin Gulf, ravaging the northern coastal provinces of Nghe An, Thanh Hoa, and Thai Binh before making landfall twelve miles west of Halong Bay. A total of 8 people were killed, 429 homes collapsed and 55,251 were damaged. About 95,000 hectares (235,000 acres) of crops were flooded.

While typhoons affect coastal regions, droughts regularly devastate inland areas. While Vietnam traditionally prepares for floods and typhoons, which are dramatic and devastating when they hit, drought is a slow, silent disaster, which in the long run can have a more profound impact on peoples' food supplies and their livelihoods.

In 2013, severe drought came to the Central Highlands.

According to the provincial Department of Labour, Invalids and Social Affairs, by the spring of 2013 nearly 34,000 people in the Central Highlands province of Gia Lai faced food shortages as a result of prolonged drought. The provincial People's Committee was forced to earmark VND6.3 billion (US$300,000) to buy more than 483 tons of rice to feed the local population. The drought, which lasted for months, also affected more than five thousand hectares of trees in the province. The hot weather dried up the provincial system of lakes, rivers, springs, and reservoirs. The drought created water shortages for irrigation, and local farmers in Ia Grai and Duc Co districts and Pleiku City struggled to irrigate their coffee and pepper crops. According to ASEAN-CN.org, coffee farms in the Central Highlands requested a second watering drive as rivers, lakes, and ponds in the region dried up. The underground water level was four to five meters lower than that in 2006. About half of the region's coffee farms were short of water.

The nation suffered through a crippling drought in 2010, when water levels in the nation's fertile rice bowl fell to their lowest points in nearly twenty years, threatening the livelihoods of tens of millions of people who depended on the river basin for farming, fishing and transportation. The biggest problem, however, was the salt. During the dry season, when channels and tributaries run dry, seawater can creep more than eighteen miles inland. Vietnam has installed a series of sluice gates to hold back high tides as well as to control annual monsoon flooding. This has allowed farmers to switch between growing rice in the wet season and raising shrimp in the brackish waters in the dry. The result has been more-effective land use and higher crop yields, and a doubling of farmers' incomes in the Delta since 1999.

As the 2010 drought intensified, in some places destructive seawater crept nearly forty miles inland.

And in 2012, drought caused an estimated loss of almost VND55 billion ($2.6 million) for Gia Lai.

"We are sitting on fire," said Nguyen Van Duyen, a farmer from Binh Phuoc Province to the west of Ho Chi Minh City, to *Thanh Nien News* in a story published on April 7, 2013. "We have been making use of all streams, digging our ponds and wells deeper, but there's still not enough water to drink, let alone to feed plants."

The province agriculture authorities said that since late December 2012 it was hot and dry in the area. Drought killed crops in 10,644 hectares of cultivation land, including 7,224 hectares of rice, causing losses of around VND75 billion (US$3.58 million) in total-a record for damage caused by drought in the province.

Unofficial statistics showed that 10,585 families, or 9.3 percent of the province's population, were in need of clean water.

According to *Thanh Nien News*, several rivers in Da Nang, the hub of the central region, were salinized, while water levels at irrigation dams dropped to thirty to fifty percent of their capacity. Starting in April, 2013, Kien Giang Water Supply Company reduced its supply by thirty percent after its reservoirs collected less water than usual. People in the coastal An Minh district said all their water sources were salinized. Many families in Dong Hung Commune, after using up rainwater from their many jars and unable to use salty water in their wells, had to buy water delivered by boats from other places at nine times more than the normal price. Some drought victims on the island district of Kien Hai turned the disaster into their own opportunity for profit by sailing their fishing boats to buy water from other places and reselling it to locals at a high markup.

Pressure on Food Production

According to the 2012 "Worldwide Population Prospects," the UN estimates that the global population will grow from 7.2 billion today to 8.1 billion in 2025. That increase of nine hundred million people in twelve years will put a significant strain on global food supplies and food trade disparity. Unfortunately, the population gain will be greatest in developing countries where domestic food production is already low and arable land is scarce. Because developing countries are often poor and lack the resources for sustainable agricultural production, they rely on global markets to provide for their food security. When global food prices spike, many poor countries do not have the resources or means to resist local inflationary pressure. This cost is passed down to the populace who cannot support the burden of the cost increase and suffer nutritional deficiencies.

Recent studies suggest that spikes in food prices tend to coincide with civil unrest, making food security vital to political stability.

The causes of food insecurity are many and complex, and the global trends are not favorable. While food production has steadily increased, it has not been enough to relieve the pressure on food supplies, particularly during natural disasters.

One element is the increasing urbanization of humanity. The year 2008 was the first time that urban populations outweighed their rural counterparts. Typical urban migrants are young, educated, and drawn to the opportunities of the big city, while rural populations are growing older and less capable of keeping pace with the increasing demands of agriculture. The migration of the young and talented has resulted in a brain drain from rural areas desperate for labor and innovation; while urban sprawl caused by that very same migration threatens rural communities worldwide.

The United Nations reports that over the last fifty years, cultivated land (permanent cropland and arable land) has grown on average one percent per year while worldwide agricultural production has averaged gains between two percent and four percent. Over that same period, the amount of cultivated land per person has declined from 0.44 hectares (about one acre) to 0.25 hectares (about two-thirds of an acre).

Worldwide agricultural production owes much of its sustained increases to irrigated farming, which has reduced the need for new arable land but has increased pressure on local water systems.

The globalization of trade and finance has given rise to a new global middle class that is increasingly shifting their diets towards higher calorie foods. Foods such as beef, fish, poultry, and dairy are becoming more commonplace in diets that traditionally consisted of more tubers and grains. Between 1990 and 2010, there was a two percent per annum increase in real per capita income. As a result, dietary energy demands increased by an average of 210 kcal per person per day.

Further complicating matters of food security is the prevalence of soil degradation and natural disasters, both of which continue to dramatically effect crop yields. Recent estimates by the International Assessment of Agricultural Knowledge, Science and Technology for Development (IAASTD) indicate that almost thirty-five percent of severely degraded land worldwide is due to agricultural activities. Erosion, desertification, and overgrazing continue to impact available land resources. Intensification of agricultural production without the increase of cultivated land in East and South Asia and the Pacific, Latin America and the Caribbean, and North America and Europe has led to increased vulnerabilities in water supplies as well as greater reliance on inputs such as potash and nitrogen. The lack of additional cultivated land in these areas is largely due to their absence of available and sustainable water sources.

The world's food supply is being directly impacted by government policy in biofuels. The United States is both the largest consumer and producer of ethanol in the world while Brazil has invested 4.5 percent of its cropland (2.7 million hectares of land area) to domestic biofuel production. According to the High Level Panel of Experts on Food Security and Nutrition (HLPE), which was established in 2010 as the science-policy interface of the UN Committee on World Food Security (CFS), worldwide biofuel production jumped from less than twenty billion liters per year in 2001 to over one hundred billion liters per year in 2011. The largest increase occurred in 2007 and 2008, and coincided with a sharp rise in food prices, followed by food riots in various developing countries.

Food Prices on the Rise

Even as food inequality remains persistent, and some nations experience a glut while others experience chronic shortage even in the absence of a natural disaster, food prices across the globe are on the rise. The *Times of India* reported that India's food inflation rate recently topped ten percent. Prices of staples and vegetables climbed dramatically from where they were a year previously. While the Prime Minister's Economic Advisory Council chairman C. Rangarajan anticipates bountiful harvests due to India's monsoon that may increase supply and lower prices, there is no guarantee.

China has also seen an increase in food prices, specifically pork, which saw a rise of sixty-eight percent over a period of ten weeks. Food price inflation has been in the double digits here as well.

The United Nations Food and Agriculture Organization price index has shown that fifty-five food commodities for export hit their highest level since tracking began over twenty years ago.

According to *The Daily Star* in Dhaka, Bangladesh, the United Nations Food and Agriculture Organization stated that recent food price hikes surpassed the levels that prompted riots in 2008 in Egypt, Cameroon, and Haiti. Sugar and meat were at their highest since its records began in 1990, but corn, rice and wheat were at their highest since 2008.

Robert B. Zoellick, the president of the World Bank, has stated that recent steps taken by the G-20 to stabilize food prices and increase supplies are a step in the right direction, although these supplies may quickly disappear in the face of an unexpected disaster, therefore causing prices to soar.

Surging food prices have proved a trigger for social protests in the past, forcing governments to cave into demands for action. They were a factor in the fall from power of Indonesia's long-term autocrat Suharto in 1998.

"Food price inflation could really go into double digits across the region and rise to such an extent that it undermines the purchasing power of households and as a result then slows consumer demand and overall economic growth," said Frederic Neumann, regional economist at HSBC in Hong Kong.

The Free Market Solution

In 2008, food riots hit over thirty countries across the globe. Between 2006 and 2008, average world prices for rice had risen by 217%, wheat by 136%, corn by 125%, and soybeans by 107%. In late April rice prices hit 24 cents per US pound, more than doubling the price in just seven months.

In that same month the *New York Times* described the depth and breadth of the crisis: "Anger is palpable across the globe. The food crisis is not only being felt among the poor but is also eroding the gains of the working and middle classes, sowing volatile levels of discontent and putting new pressures on fragile governments."

In Cairo, soldiers were put to work baking bread as rising food prices threatened to become the spark that ignited wider anger at the repressive Mubarak government. In Burkina Faso and other parts of Sub-Saharan Africa, food riots broke out as never before. In reasonably prosperous Malaysia, the ruling coalition was nearly ousted by voters who cited food and fuel price increases as their main concerns.

In Thailand, which produces ten million more tons of rice than it consumes and is the world's largest rice exporter, supermarkets placed signs limiting the amount of rice shoppers were allowed to purchase.

In Senegal, one of Africa's oldest and most stable democracies, police in riot gear beat and used tear gas against people protesting high food prices and later raided a television station that broadcast images of the event.

In India, people scrimped on milk for their children. Daily bowls of dal (the ubiquitous thick stew of dried lentils, peas, or beans) got thinner, as a bag of lentils was stretched across a few more meals.

In Haiti, where three-quarters of the population earns less than two dollars a day and one in five children is chronically malnourished, the one business booming amid all the gloom was the selling of patties made of mud, oil and sugar, typically consumed only by the most destitute. Yes; human beings are sometimes reduced to eating mud.

Real solutions will take years. Haiti, its agriculture industry in shambles, needs to better feed itself. Outside investment is the key, although that requires stability, not the sort of widespread looting and violence that the Haitian food riots have fostered.

Many analysts have been quick to claim that we should expect similar behavior in the future if there are not some reforms in how resources are allocated. This is true; and what is needed is a more fluid flow of food across the globe, and this can come only with free markets that are truly free.

A free market system is not what we have at the moment. Protectionist trade measures and food subsidies distort the market and make it susceptible to the sort of behavior that the food market experienced in 2008. Producers cannot accurately price their crops according to quality, and consumers either pay too much or make decisions forced upon them by governments. Subsidies often serve to keep the price of products like corn artificially high, something we should be against if we want to reduce global poverty.

Even fair trade schemes that claim to help sustainable and ethical farming can sometimes cause those who cannot afford to meet these standards to be worse off. The false dichotomy between capitalism and humanitarianism is hugely detrimental to the alleviation of misery around the world. Technology will continue to lower the price of food production and transport. It is up to government to decide if they want to support such progress or not.

The Global Food Exchange™ Fills a Market Void

We are seeing global food demand increase without a corresponding increase in relative supply. This is caused by both the need for short-term emergency supplies and because of overall long-term pressure on food production. These needs are not currently being met by government programs or existing free market solutions. There is a clear void that needs to be filled.

Short-term needs are urgent. During the past decade, in the aftermath of natural disasters more than 1,800,000 people have died as a result of inadequate food and unclean water. Even in the United States we are seeing an increase on the number and severity of natural disasters. As recently as October of 2012, leading organizations including Munich-Re, the world's largest insurer, have published reports announcing grave concerns that trends suggest the United States is likely to suffer more great natural disasters in the coming decades.

In the first few days or even weeks after these horrible events, often only a very small fraction of the needed relief supplies are actually available to be delivered to the affected sites.

Long-term problems persist, and they take many forms.

Food technology has flattened over the past fifteen years. Where new seeds or fertilizers or soil preparations have historically helped increase the yield per acre decade after decade, which has helped offset increasing demand, there have not been any major improvements in this century. Primary food crops like corn are promoted as alternative fuels. This decreases the amount of corn for use as food, which drives food prices up.

Increasing energy prices also drive up food prices. Oil and gas are needed to produce, harvest, and transport crops. When energy prices go up, food prices go up.

Then there is the rising risk of massive crop loss caused by the lack of diversity among crops. Where there were more than eighty types of wheat several decades ago, there are now only a handful that comprise the majority of the world's wheat harvest, leaving huge percentages of the world's wheat at risk should one bacteria or virus or pest break through.

There are many other factors, and perhaps the most troubling one continues to be the loss of critical elements in the world's soils. Because of overuse, active erosion, and other causes, the nutritional value of food is on the decline, and health related problems caused by chronically poor nutrition are well-known.

The Global Food Exchange™ was created as a solution to two great problems plaguing the world today. Through the securitization of long-term food storage and a strategic storage network, the GFE has taken the world's most valuable commodity, food, and given qualified investors the ability to invest in an asset class that is less susceptible to the risks of most every other asset class while at the same time making lifesaving supplies available to those in need following natural disasters.

Why is GFE a logical answer?

One reason is that food prices, which typically rise dramatically in times surrounding natural disasters, can be stabilized through a schedule of regular advance purchasing. Resolving this inefficiency can provide solid returns for investors while saving millions of lives that otherwise are lost.

When making a purchase for disaster relief, governments generally consider the following three factors in this order:

1. Quantity is the most important factor, as governments and NGOs prefer working with the fewest number of vendors possible. As the GFE continues to build its stored volume, it will be a primary resource for FEMA, USAID, OFDA, the UN, World Vision, and others.

2. Location is also critical for post-disaster relief. In the first critical days following a disaster, containers of food or water filtration systems are useless if they must be shipped thousands of miles. Government agencies such as the Federal Emergency Management Agency (FEMA) and non-profits like the Red Cross and the Salvation Army have very limited amounts of stored food, and it's often not enough to meet the sudden demand a natural disaster creates. They don't store food in as many locations as GFE intends to eventually have supplies. Many agencies see GFE as the solution to their inability to strategically store the needed disaster relief supplies they'll count on in a world of increasing natural disasters.

3. Price is a factor too. Because lives are at stake and a swift response is essential, quantity and location will always trump price. However, as the largest volume provider, GFE intends to maintain competitive pricing through a regular purchasing schedule from an expanding group of global manufacturers and partnerships with host companies. And to

ensure that the Global Food Exchange™ maintains its benevolent purpose, it has instituted a fixed margin approach to its business model. The GFE acts as a manufacturer and master distributor in turn selling and leasing products directly through a global network of Distributors at a fixed margin. The fixed margin is a key factor in the business design, as it prevents there ever being any potential for the company to take advantage of buyers when disaster strikes. Moreover, this business model gives partners, NGOs and relief agencies the confidence they want and need from a system that can be relied on as a one- stop solution for product sourcing. To ensure that this fixed margin remains intact, GFE provides Distributors 100% transparency of its costs.

And while quantity, location, and price are the primary factors in decision-making, having a relationship with those organizations that actually do the buying is just as important.

For example, CH2MHill is a global leader in consulting, design, design-build, operations, and program management. The company is the primary designer of disaster management plans for the US as well as individual states, and is also the single largest service provider for post-disaster provider FEMA following natural disasters. When a disaster occurs in the United States, FEMA notifies CH2MHill with active disaster plans to direct the acquisition of goods and services needed.

GFE is pleased to have the former COO for CH2MHill on the GFE board. In addition to helping GFE become a recognized provider for food, water and shelter, the organization is well advised on how to best design and package supplies to fit the needs of governments and NGOs that have feet-on-the-ground distribution expertise.

The response to GFE from foreign governments, national disaster response agencies, and the companies that manage their risk has been overwhelmingly supportive. The Board of Advisors of the Global Food Exchange™ includes current and former leaders from organizations such as World Vision, CH2MHill, and the Institute of Medicine, to name a few. The concept has been so well received that GFE has already entertained several conversations with global leaders including decision makers at FEMA, USAID, OFDA, Food For Peace, and more.

There is no high-risk environment quite like a humanitarian emergency. When disaster strikes, a fast and effective response is required. The chances of getting things wrong often times outweigh the chance of getting things right.

Therefore, there is need for a greater tolerance for risk in such situations.

But even greater risk exists in either doing nothing or in having a delayed response. These emergencies become high-risk due to the involvement of life and death situations. Loss of lives and opportunities happen because of lack of reaction and slow decision-making.

As Lord Paddy Ashdown pointed out in the *Humanitarian Emergency Response Review*, politically, being accused of letting people die is a much worse outcome than a messy response or an accusation of waste.

By having strategic partners throughout the world that supply emergency food, temporary shelter, portable water systems, and deployable power solutions, the Global Food Exchange™ is the answer to getting the right provisions to the right people at the right time. GFE's logistical system is designed for shipping specially packaged food for rapid deployment into the world's most susceptible geographic regions. GFE is committed to creating the most comprehensive network of secure food storage in the world with one focus: to serve those in immediate need following an emergency and for as long after as is required.

The GFE Key: Freeze-Dried and Dehydrated Food

What makes the GFE concept so powerful? Why now, and not ten or twenty years ago? One critical element that allows the GFE concept to work is freeze-drying.

Nearly every industry over the last decade has made huge strides in the production and quality of products. The technology that makes possible freeze-dried food has likewise made vast improvements in both the quality and variety of food now offered by the freeze-dried food industry. The current trend of emergency food storage in America has brought about a tremendous increase in the number of freeze-dried food manufacturers as well as many innovative improvements to how the product is made.

Many of us recall our first experience with freeze-dried food as a meal while camping, probably decades ago. We enjoyed its convenience when a kitchen was not available, or considered freeze-dried meals an edible substitute when we were in the middle of the wilderness and had to carry our own food. But it certainly wasn't the kind of meal we would want every day, much less three times a day, for weeks or months on end. The problem of excessive salt found in traditional meals ready to eat (MREs) dramatically increases gastrointestinal distress and the need for much higher quantities which are often shipped separately.

But those days have changed.

Extensive research and testing has revealed that some foods are better when preserved using the freeze-drying process and some foods reconstitute better after being dehydrated. The key that allows the highest quality in taste, texture and nutritional value is getting those combinations right.

Most of what people used over the years for camping had a shelf life of two or three years, but technology developed over the past decade using multi-layer Mylar bags and nitrogen-filled bags allows freeze-dried food to be stored in temperature moderated areas for up to twenty-five years. Rather than storing food by traditional means, full of water and heavy packaging, the freeze-drying method allows for the substantial volume of water normally contained in food to be added at the site using water filtration systems. These portable water filtration systems serve multiple purposes including the rehydration of food, the provision of clean drinking water, and even sufficient water for light bathing. Moreover, the space needed for portable water filtration systems is a fraction of the room the water itself would take, meaning significantly more nutrition can be shipped in each container.

The process of freeze-drying food consists of a detailed set of steps that includes high temperatures, intense amounts of pressure and time. Here's a quick overview of what happens during the freeze-dried food production process.

Most foods require some prep work before they can be frozen. It would be nearly impossible to freeze-dry a whole potato or an entire chicken breast! Some foods like fish, poultry, and beef also need to be cooked before the process can begin. Many of the products purchased by freeze-dried food producers have already gone through some of the prep work, but products are always checked for spoilage, bacterial counts, contamination, and purity before they ever enter the freeze-drying process.

After the food has been prepared and tested, it is laid out flat on large metal trays, which are then positioned into large, wheeled carts. These carts are then typically placed in a massive walk-in freezer where the temperature may be set as low as minus forty degrees Fahrenheit. The extreme temperature freezes the food quickly, and the carts remain in the freezer for a pre-determined period of time before they are transferred to a drying chamber.

The drying chambers are generally long, depressurized chambers that expose the now-frozen food products to a process called sublimation. This intensive process is a combination of using a vacuum to greatly reduce the pressure in the chamber and heat conduction, radiation or microwave heat to raise the temperature of the food to about one hundred degrees. The combination of the extreme heat and vacuum turns the ice crystals in the food into water vapor before the liquid has a chance to melt, at which point the moisture is pulled away from the food and condensed in the depressurized chamber.

This process allows the food to keep its original color and shape, while the pores created from the extracted ice crystals make rehydrating the food as easy as reintroducing water. In the end, roughly ninety-eight percent of the water is removed from food during this process.

The result is an innovative product that when packaged sufficiently can maintain a shelf life of up to twenty-five years. In some cases, the nutrition delivered in these meals is higher than the victim's traditional pre-disaster diet. This combination of concentrating tremendous amounts of nutrition into lightweight and long-shelf-life food gives the Global Food Exchange™ one of the most important advantages needed to bring relief to disaster victims.

The Food Relief Vault™

For the GFE concept to work, freeze-dried food must be stored in large amounts in containers that are durable, secure, and easy to ship over long distances.

The solution is the Food Relief Vault™, which is an ISO certified shipping container filled with freeze-dried meals that can feed 650 adults three meals per day over the course of thirty days. This Relief Vault is maintained in secure locations, which are outfitted with fences, remote cameras, and even custom devices to monitor temperature, humidity, and movement. All containers are fully insured.

GFE has several US locations selected for storage and they are near but not necessarily in the disaster zones. For example, Houston, Texas is one of the highest risk areas, and to serve that part of the US, Relief Vaults are located in West Texas. The demands of the Southeastern corridor are met with storage in central Georgia.

In addition to the predictions of increased natural disaster events in the United States by Munich-Re and other disaster trend analysts, a primary reason for working from North

America and South America and then to Europe as Phase I is to build critical stores of food in the world's safest areas before venturing into areas requiring more advanced security strategies.

In instances where the strategic location may be politically unstable, GFE partners with US AID, the UN, the Red Cross or other local parties who have an established, secure base of operations. This keeps the cost of storage down while providing optimal security.

To meet regional diet customs, GFE provides customized meals for various regions of the world. The combination of cereals, pastas, fruits, vegetables, and drinks are very similar for Europe, the Middle East and the Americas, but in Asia where there is very little dairy in the diet, meals have been modified to reflect more rice and protein and no dairy. In Africa, where complex foods are not easily digested, wheat and rice based crackers replace pastas, and powdered yogurts are the basis for most meals.

The GFE website is constantly being updated on the efforts underway to get aid to the victims. Until now, very little has changed over the last fifty years in how the world delivers aid to these victims. The mission of GFE is to save lives through rapid delivery of the needed relief supplies. Investors enjoy making a difference in the lives of these victims as much as they enjoy the potential profits.

Three Additional Relief Vault Types

In addition to the Food Relief Vault™, GFE distributes and trades three additional types of Relief Vaults.

The GFE recognizes that safe drinking water is an essential item following any disaster, and it's GFE's goal to provide all forms of clean water solutions to those in need. A Water Relief Vault™, or WRV, is an ISO shipping container specially designed to house 100,000 gallon per day (gpd) high-tech Industrial Reverse Osmosis System (IROS) with integrated diesel generator sets, and containerized desalination systems. These systems come with trained operators, and are available through a monthly lease program.

Shelter Relief Vault™ (SRV) is also an ISO container with either Premium or Basic Shelter systems included. Premium Shelters are high quality FEMA and US military approved designs, which include solar panels on the roof, bunk beds, and partition walls.

Basic Shelters are ergonomically designed domed shelters that include hammocks for sleeping and storage space.

Combination Relief Vault™ (CRV) is an ISO shipping container that combines food, water and shelter into one self-sustaining container. The CRV is intended either for remote incidents where complete support is needed for smaller groups or where the populations of a large disaster require numerous decentralized relief centers.

The Global Food Exchange™ team is also expecting to launch partnerships for rapid set up mobile hospitals in 2014.

Food as an Investment Asset

The GFE Relief Vault concept is one whose time has come for disaster relief. The idea of preparing, storing, and then warehousing thousands of freeze-dried meals in global locations that are quickly accessible makes perfect sense. The technology exists to make it happen.

The humanitarian value of the GFE Relief Vault is clear. But how does a free market model make this a long-term solution, and what about its investment potential?

The trends are positive.

When compared to most other investable assets such as stocks, bonds, currencies, and even precious metals, food is arguably the most valuable commodity in the world. Does anyone believe food prices won't be higher in ten years than they are now? Further research would suggest that on a risk-adjusted basis, long-term food stores should not only be considered an independent asset class, but an integral asset for those pursuing more reliable portfolio returns and more truly non-correlated assets.

What defines an asset class? How do we decide on which asset class to use?

An asset class is a group of securities that exhibit similar characteristics, behave similarly in the marketplace, and are subject to the same laws and regulations. The three traditional asset classes are equities (stocks), fixed-income (bonds) and cash equivalents (money market instruments). Whatever the asset class lineup, each one is expected to reflect different risk and return investment characteristics and will perform differently in any given market environment.

In addition to the three traditional asset classes, some investment professionals have added real estate and commodities to the asset class mix.

Let's discuss commodities. Commodities are the raw materials humans use to create a livable world. Humans use energy to sustain themselves, metals to build weapons and tools, and agricultural products including livestock and farm products to feed themselves. These are the four traditional classes of commodities, and they are the essential building blocks of the global economy.

1. Energy (including crude oil, heating oil, natural gas and gasoline)

2. Metals (including gold, silver, platinum and copper)

3. Livestock and meat (including lean hogs, pork bellies, live cattle and feeder cattle)

4. Agricultural (including corn, soybeans, wheat, rice, cocoa, coffee, cotton and sugar)

Ancient civilizations traded a wide array of commodities, including livestock, seashells, spices and gold. Although the quality of product, date of delivery, and transportation methods were often unreliable, commodity trading was an essential business. Down through the centuries and to this day, the prosperity of a nation is directly proportionate to its ability to create and manage complex trading systems and facilitate commodity trades, as these serve as the wheels of commerce, economic development, and taxation. Today as then, reputation and reliability are critical underpinnings to secure the trust of investors, traders and suppliers.

Commodities generally meet the following three criteria.

The commodity has to be *tradable*, meaning there needs to be a viable investment vehicle to help investors trade it. For example, a commodity is included if it has a futures contract assigned to it on one of the major exchanges, or if a company processes it, or if there's an exchange traded fund (ETF) that tracks it.

All commodities have to be physically *deliverable*. Wheat is included because it can be delivered by the bushel, and crude oil is included because it can be delivered in barrels.

Every commodity market needs *liquidity* and an active market with buyers and sellers constantly transacting with each other. Liquidity is critical because it gives investors the option of getting in and out of an investment without having to face the difficulty of trying to find a buyer or seller for their securities. Commodities are standardized goods that have a universal price around the world. Gold, for example, has the same price per ounce in Brazil as it does in Bombay, whereas the price of a television set or a pair of shoes varies depending on the brand and the place in which it is sold.

Commodity trading in the exchanges requires agreed-upon standards so that trades can be executed without visual inspection. You don't want to buy ten thousand units of pork bellies only to find out that the meat is diseased, or discover that the corn you purchased is of inferior or unacceptable quality.

Global economic development, technological advances, and market demands for commodities influence the prices of staples such as oil, aluminum, copper, sugar and corn. For instance, the emergence of China and India as significant economic players has contributed to the declining availability and higher prices of industrial metals, such as steel, for the rest of the globe.

Basic economic principles typically control the commodities markets: lower supply equals higher prices. Major disruptions in supply, such as widespread health scares, diseases, drought, or other reasons for lower production can lead to investing plays, given that the long-term demand for food commodities is generally stable and predictable.

For example, the severe drought that swept through much of the United States in 2012 continued into 2013, threatening to cripple economic growth while forcing consumers to pay higher food prices. The drought had a significant impact on prices, especially beef, pork and chicken. The severe weather put nearly eighty percent of the continental United States in drought conditions that were the worst in fifty years. Particularly hard hit areas included the mid-western states of Illinois, Iowa, Minnesota, Nebraska, Kansas, as well as Oklahoma, Texas, Arkansas and many parts of Colorado and California. The drought ruined key crops like corn, wheat, and soybeans, driving up commodity prices. Farmers were forced to cut back on the number of livestock in order to limit their own costs and so created a shortage of beef, chicken, and pork. According to the US Drought Monitor, during the summer of 2013, while drought conditions eased in some areas, roughly sixty percent of the country still suffered from drought, which remained at its worst levels in more than a decade.

Futures, forward contracts, and hedging are a prevalent practice with commodities. The airline sector is a classic example of a large industry that, for long-range planning purposes, must secure enormous amounts of fuel at stable prices. Airline companies therefore engage in hedging and purchase fuel futures at fixed rates in order to avoid market volatility. Farming cooperatives also utilize this mechanism. Without futures and hedging, volatility in commodities could cause bankruptcies for businesses that require predictability in managing their expenses. Commodity exchanges are used by manufacturers and service providers as part of their budgeting process; the ability to stabilize costs through the use of forward contracts reduces expense volatility. There are no forward contracts, options or futures available through the Global Food Exchange™ as it presently acts as a manufacturer only, though the demand for such contracts is expected to grow in the future.

Commodities investments have a degree of volatility because they are affected by external forces that are difficult, if not impossible, to predict. These include natural disasters, erratic weather patterns, and manmade disasters.

With commodities playing a major and critical role in the global economic markets and affecting the lives of most of the people on the planet, there are multitudes of commodity and futures exchanges around the world. Each exchange carries a few commodities or specializes in a single commodity. For instance, the US Futures Exchange is an important exchange that only carries energy commodities.

The most popular exchanges include the CME Group, which resulted after the Chicago Mercantile Exchange and Chicago Board of Trade merged in 2006, Intercontinental Exchange, Kansas City Board of Trade, and the London Metal Exchange.

Founded in 1898 as the Chicago Butter and Egg Board, an agricultural commodities exchange, the CME Group is the leading American commodities exchange. Today, the CME (or "Merc") trades several types of financial instruments: interest rates, equities, currencies, and commodities. Agricultural commodity contracts include: live cattle, lean hogs, feeder cattle, class IV milk, class III milk, frozen pork bellies, international skimmed milk powder (ISM), nonfat dry milk, deliverable nonfat dry milk, dry whey, cash-settled butter, butter, random length lumber, softwood pulp, and hardwood pulp. It also offers trading in alternative investments, such as weather and real estate derivatives, and has the largest options and futures contracts open interest (number of contracts outstanding) of any futures exchange in the world.

In the last five years, alternative investments have seen an investment growth rate seven times that of traditional asset classes. If food were distributed as an asset class, it would fit right beside alternative investments as a substitute for other securities and investment opportunities. The global debt crisis has caused significant instability within financial markets as equities continue to wear on investor trust, and safe assets like government bonds and notes return historically low yields. Some of the world's largest funds are ditching equity and commodity markets for less volatile investments that provide comparable returns.

Investors have been finding that on a risk-adjusted basis returns have been dwindling for more than a decade. Even assets like bonds are no longer producing respectable or safe returns. Forty years ago, bonds were generally accepted as the asset class to be used in an investment portfolio to reduce volatility by acting as a "non-correlated asset" when paired with stocks. This is no longer the case. A preponderance of US government bonds are owned by foreign investors like China, and when they decide to sell their US assets, they sell stocks and bonds together. And while the central banks hold interest rates down to soften the blow of their own interest obligations, they continue to print money, creating a fundamentally weaker currency. The long-term effects of this monetary easing are always a rise in core commodity prices.

Bond values and rates of return are now as volatile as many of their equity counterparts, making them undesirable for investors who have looked to bonds for their safety and consistency of returns.

Food is different. Until now, there have never been any long-term securities that truly reflected the cost of consumer foods. No one likes that food prices have been steadily going up for years, but for an investor it becomes a great benefit. During the most tragic markets, food prices have steadily continued their rise. Over the past decade government bond returns have followed interest rates as they have spiraled downward, setting new lows, while food prices have marched upward almost as dramatically.

The risk of companies not being able to service their debt has been on the rise. The only thing that may outpace that change in risk is the risk held by investing in sovereign and municipal debt. When compared side-by-side on a risk-adjusted basis, consumer food prices have not only proven to be less volatile, but as an asset class returns have been more than triple that of US government bonds.

Food is one of the best investments available on a risk-adjusted basis for investors. With an investment in food, a portfolio has a standardized hedge against rising food prices. Investing in food as an asset class is unique to any investment that has ever been securitized.

It is not the same as investing in traditional commodities, because such investments are not a time reflection of food prices in aggregate. In commodity options and futures you do not just pay for the underlying asset, you pay a premium set by the seller based on calendar risk set to lock in your price.

In its simplest form, the GFE acts as a manufacturer that in turn offers access to Agents or Distributors some of which are public or private funds that wish to purchase food as an asset class. The two primary assets purchased for investment include: Food Relief Vaults™, the forty-foot containers filled with food specially packaged for a shelf life of up to twenty-five years, and Water Relief Vaults™, containing industrial water filtration systems designed for disaster relief at wholesale prices. These funds earn a profit by selling the Relief Vaults to governmental and non-governmental relief agencies at a profit either directly or on the electronic Global Food Exchange™ platform.

Now with food securitized and traded as an asset class, the world's most valuable commodity can bring stability and returns back to any investment portfolio.

The challenges facing us in terms of demand for food production, distribution, and access to food as well as environmental obstacles create upward pressure on food prices.

One may reasonably expect, in the assimilation of the modern portfolio, for investments in food as an asset to replace bond investments. Savvy investors will recognize that food has the risk profile of bonds, but with upwards return potential on par with equity investments. Here is the dichotomy; food is an ideal investment for investors of all ages and investment horizons. Whether you're a young investor seeking high returns or a seasoned investor fleeing to safer investments, food can be a very rational investment. Whether your investment portfolio has a short-term or long-term expected holding period, food can be a rational investment.

The Global Food Exchange™ has found what it believes, and what experts believe, to be a solution to one of the world's most dire problems: More efficient disaster relief efforts that save lives, coupled with the potential for a return to investors. It's doing well by doing good. By accessing the capital markets, the company hopes to advance the interest of free market solutions and elicit creative ideas to solve other dire problems facing the world. For more information please check out GlobalFoodExchange.Org.

Chapter Six: Looking Ahead

What does the future hold?

One thing is certain: unless we can somehow exchange planet Earth for an upgraded model, life on our beloved rocky sphere will be characterized by the same challenges that we've faced for thousands of years: how to provide ourselves with food, water, shelter, and energy while minimizing the impact of environmental assaults including earthquakes, floods, droughts, and storms. Regardless of climate change or the politics of the day, these problems are not going to go away. Summer or winter, fair weather or foul, rising or falling tides—the earth will always be a dynamic system, constantly changing, forever unsettled. Somewhere, a village will have too little food. A town will be destroyed by an earthquake. A volcano will spew toxic ash over a city. A prolonged drought will precede a torrential flood.

The past is prelude.

During the twentieth century, an estimated seventy million people died of starvation across the world. This is a number greater than the current combined populations of California and Texas.

Thirty million died during the famine of 1958–61 in China. Other horrific famines of the century included famines in China in 1928 and 1942, and the 1942–1945 disaster in Bengal. Several famines struck the Soviet Union, including the great famine of 1932-1933, which was created by the government's forced collectivization of agriculture. Later in the century saw the Biafra famine in the 1960s, the Khmer Rouge-induced famine in Cambodia in the 1970s, the Ethiopian famine of 1984–85, and the North Korean famine of the 1990s.

In the middle of the twentieth century, when the world's population was around half what it is now, the answer to looming famines was the Green Revolution—a massive increase in the use of chemical fertilizers and hybrid seeds.

It seemed to work. Between 1950 and 1984, hybrid strains of high-yielding crops transformed agriculture around the globe and world grain production nearly tripled.

By the late 1980s, food production seemed sufficient. In earlier decades a third of the population in the developing world had been undernourished. By the tail end of the Green Revolution, the share had fallen below twenty percent, and the absolute number of hungry people dipped below eight hundred million for the first time in modern history. Governments and foundations responded by cutting back on agricultural research, or redirecting money into the problems created by intensive farming, like environmental damage. According to the *New York Times*, over a twenty-year period Western aid for agricultural development in poor countries fell by almost half, with mass layoffs at some of the world's most important research centers.

Some experts criticized the Green Revolution and asserted that these new high-yielding crops require more chemical fertilizers and pesticides, which harm the environment. Although these high-yielding crops have made it possible to feed more people, there are signs that regional food production has peaked in many world sectors, as the result of strategies associated with intensive agriculture including groundwater over-drafting and overuse of pesticides and other agricultural chemicals.

Unfortunately, food production leveled off just as food and feed demand was starting to increase, in part due to rising affluence across much of Asia. Millions of people added meat and dairy products to their diets, requiring increased amounts of grain to be produced. At the same time, much of the American corn crop was converted into ethanol.

Erratic weather drove down yields. A 2003 heat wave in Europe, that some researchers believe was worsened by climate change, cut agricultural output in some countries by as much as thirty percent. A sustained drought in Australia cut rice and wheat production.

For much of the twenty-first century, consumption of the four staples that supply most human calories—wheat, rice, corn and soybeans—has outpaced production, drawing once-large stockpiles down to dangerous levels. The imbalance between supply and demand has resulted in two huge spikes in international grain prices since 2007, with some grains more than doubling in cost.

While felt only moderately in the industrialized West, the price jumps worsened hunger for tens of millions of poor people, and even destabilized politics in dozens of countries. Nations began hoarding food, and panic buying ensued in some markets, particularly for rice. Food riots broke out in more than thirty countries. The Haitian government was ousted in 2008 amid food riots, and anger over high prices played a role in the uprisings of the Arab Spring.

Healthy harvests in 2008 and 2009 helped rebuild stocks, and that factor, combined with the global recession, drove prices down in 2009. But then more weather-related harvest failures sent them soaring again.

Experts are warning that the era of cheap food may be over. "Our mindset was surpluses," said Dan Glickman, a former United States secretary of agriculture. "That has just changed overnight." Recent price spikes have helped cause the largest increases in world hunger in decades. In 2012 the Food and Agriculture Organization of the United Nations estimated the number of hungry people has increased from below 800 million to 925 million. The World Bank says the current figure could be as high as 940 million.

In estimating whether food production can keep pace with consumption, the most critical part of the equation is population growth.

In their 2012 Worldwide Population Prospects, the UN estimated that the global population would grow from 7.2 billion in 2013 to 8.1 billion in 2025. That increase of nine hundred million people in twelve years is expected to put a significant strain on global food supplies and food inequity.

By 2050, it's estimated that there will be over nine billion people on earth.

Unfortunately, population gains will be greatest in developing countries where domestic food and arable land is scarce. Because developing countries are often poor and lack the resources for sustainable agricultural production, they rely on global markets to provide for their food security. When global food prices spike, many poor countries do not have the resources or means to resist local inflationary pressure. This cost is passed down to the populace who cannot afford the cost increase and suffer nutritional deficiencies.

Studies indicate that increases in food prices tend to coincide with civil unrest, making food security vital to political stability.

Water Shortages

Most of the three billion people projected to be added worldwide by mid-century will be born in countries already experiencing water shortages. In scores of countries, including Northern China, the United States, and India, water tables are falling due to widespread over-pumping. Other countries including Pakistan, Iran, and Mexico will eventually experience water scarcity and reduced grain harvest. Water deficits, which are already spurring heavy grain imports in numerous smaller countries, may soon do the same in larger countries, such as China or India. Even with the over-pumping of its aquifers, China has developed a grain deficit, contributing to the upward pressure on grain prices.

After China and India, a second group of smaller countries also have significant water deficits—Algeria, Egypt, Iran, Mexico, and Pakistan. Four of these already import a large share of their grain. Only Pakistan remains self-sufficient, but with a population expanding by four million a year, it will also soon seek grain on the world market.

According to a UN climate report, as both temperatures and human demand rise, the Himalayan glaciers that are the principal dry-season water sources of Asia's biggest rivers—Ganges, Indus, Brahmaputra, Yangtze, Mekong, Salween and Yellow—could disappear by 2350. Approximately 2.4 billion people live in the drainage basin of the Himalayan rivers. In India alone, the Ganges provides water for drinking and farming for more than five hundred million people. In coming decades, India, China, Pakistan, Afghanistan, Bangladesh, Nepal, and Myanmar could experience floods followed by severe droughts.

Booming cities are urbanizing agricultural land and competing with farmers for water. In some of the world's breadbaskets, farmers have achieved high output only by pumping groundwater much faster than nature can replenish it.

Environmental Challenges

Many of the failed harvests of the twenty-first century have been a consequence of weather disasters, like floods in the United States, drought in Australia, and blistering heat waves in Europe and Russia. In some of the most important agricultural countries, temperatures are rising rapidly during the growing season.

Professor Andrew Challinor, from the University of Leeds' School of Earth and Environment, said in the journal *Global Change Biology*, "Feeding a growing population as climate changes is a major challenge, especially since the land available for agricultural expansion is limited. Supplies of the major food crops could be at risk unless we plan for future climates."

Dr. Ed Hawkins from the National Centre for Atmospheric Science (NCAS) at the University of Reading said, "Our research rings alarm bells for future food security. Over the last fifty years, developments in agriculture, such as fertilizers and irrigation, have increased yields of the world's staple foods, but we're starting to see a slowdown in yield increases. Our research into maize suggests the increasing frequency of hot days across the world might explain some of this slowdown.

"We expect hot days to become more frequent still, and our work on maize suggests that current advances in agriculture are too slow to offset the expected damage to crops from heat stress in the future."

Does the difference of a few degrees matter when growing maize or, for that matter, any other food crop? You'd think that as long as the plants had enough water, they'd like the extra heat.

Not so. Researchers have found that over the last fifty years, yields of maize in France have become more sensitive to temperature. In some parts of France, during the last fifty years the number of days with temperatures over 32°C (89.6° F) has more than doubled. Many other land areas show similar increases. By the 2020s, temperatures over 32°C could occur over large areas of France where previously they were uncommon. Without agricultural development, this increase in hot days could *decrease* yields of French maize by more than ten percent relative to current yield.

Even if we have another multi-year cold wave, the change or volatility in the environment could be detrimental to those plants that have grown more accustomed to higher seasonal temperatures. Volatility in climate trends may be more dangerous to food security than slow trends.

The Future: Challenge and Hope

Experts say that in coming decades, in order to keep pace with global consumption the world's farmers need to do three things:

1. Withstand whatever climate volatility comes their way
2. Double the amount of food they produce to meet rising demand
3. Reduce the environmental damage caused by the business of agriculture

Agronomists emphasize that the situation is far from hopeless. Examples are already available, from the rice paddies of India to the deserts of Mexico, to show that it may be possible to make agriculture more productive and more resilient in the face of climate volatility. Farmers have achieved huge gains in output in the past, and rising prices are a powerful incentive to do so again.

But new crop varieties and new techniques are required, far beyond those available now, scientists have said. Leading researchers say it is possible to create crop varieties that are more resistant to drought and flooding and that respond especially well to rising carbon dioxide. The scientists are less certain that crops can be made to withstand withering heat, though genetic engineering may eventually make it possible.

Perhaps the most hopeful sign nowadays is that poor countries themselves are starting to invest in agriculture in a serious way, as many did not do in the years when food was cheap.

In Africa, largely bypassed by the Green Revolution but with enormous potential, a dozen countries are on the verge of fulfilling a promise to devote ten percent of their budgets to farm development, up from five percent or less.

"In my country, every penny counts," Agnes Kalibata, the agriculture minister of Rwanda, said in an interview with the *New York Times*. With difficulty, Rwanda has met the ten percent pledge, and she cited a terracing project in the country's highlands that has raised potato yields by six hundred percent for some farmers.

Yet poor countries cannot solve the problems by themselves. Coupled with the demand for diets richer in protein, current population projections mean that food production may need to double by later in the century. That demand must somehow be met on a planet where little new land is available for farming, where fresh water supplies are dwindling, where the weather has become erratic, and where the food system is already showing serious signs of stress. Agriculture is a leading threat to rivers, lakes, and coastal environments, and up to forty percent of all cropland worldwide is experiencing soil erosion, reduced fertility, or overgrazing. As our climate changes, so will the ways we grow our food. Fortunately, many people are working on ways to produce more healthy and delicious food while sustaining the environment.

Here are some trends and new ideas that may help avert famine in the future. How many of them will be effective? Let's hope the free markets will be allowed to decide.

More Efficient Farms

All over the tropics, forests are being converted to pastures and farmland: eighty percent of all new tropical farmland is created by replacing forests, with huge environmental costs. But we could produce fifty percent more food without new farmland by increasing yields, shifting diets, and using water and fertilizer more efficiently.

Perennial Grains

Most farm crops, including wheat, rice, and maize, are annuals, and must be newly planted every year. The roots of these annual plants are shallow, and farmers often use resource-intensive cultivation practices to grow them. But many wild plants, such as wheatgrass, are perennials that live several years and produce food over many seasons. Their roots are extensive and they help stabilize and build healthy soils.

Vertical Farming

Feeding the growing global population using current methods would require immense amounts of agricultural land that we don't have. But seventy percent of people will live in cities. Urban farms can be found today in yards, roofs, and balconies.

Advanced Fish Farms

Promising new methods of farming fish rely on giant tanks. Water, nutrients, and waste are recycled—sometimes to grow plants—and fish can't escape. Such methods could relieve pressure on wild stocks drastically depleted by overfishing. And closed-system fish farms don't have the same environmental downsides as open cage or pen fish farms, which use more wild fish for feed and can cause pollution and disease.

Underutilized Species

About 2,500 plant species have been domesticated for food. But today, almost half our food calories come from just three grains: wheat, maize, and rice. The thousands of overlooked plant species—and untapped diversity of animals—could provide solutions to problems like the need for resilience in our food production systems and the need to meet growing demands without depleting natural resources.

Here are a few promising examples.

138

• Algae: Already popular in Japan, seaweed and other algae are highly nutritious and can be grown in both fresh water and salt water. Some in the sustainable food industry predict algae farming could become the world's biggest cropping industry. It has long been a staple in Asia and many countries including Japan have huge farms. One of seaweed's useful qualities is that it grows at a phenomenal rate—it's the fastest growing plant on earth.

• Insects: Over two thousand species of insects are already eaten worldwide. Insects are high in protein and require much less land, water, and food than animals raised for meat. Because insects are cold-blooded, they have a high food conversion rate, meaning they eat far less than livestock like cattle. Ten kilograms (twenty-two pounds) of feed yields six to eight kilograms of insect meat compared to just one kilogram of beef. Insects are abundant, produce less greenhouse gas and manure, and when eaten do not transfer any diseases that can mutate into a dangerous human form.

A large percentage of the world's population already eats insects as a regular part of their diet. Caterpillars and locusts are popular in Africa, wasps are a delicacy in Japan, and crickets are eaten in Thailand.

• Minor millets: These cereals have been grown in Asia for thousands of years. Many farmers in India and Nepal are now switching from growing crops like maize and rice back to traditional varieties bred to grow on local mountainsides.

• Quinoa: This grain from the Andes contains all the essential amino acids the human body needs for protein and has no gluten.

• Emmer wheat: While millions are spent on high-tech hybrids, neglected crops like the grain emmer require less fertilizer and fewer pesticides than currently used breeds.

• Giant swamp taro: Rich in vitamins and minerals, the giant swamp taro grows well in the salty, sandy soil of many Pacific islands. Yellow varieties are high in beta carotene.

• Peach palm: The peach palm grows well in Central and South America and produces a large, nutritious fruit. The tree's spiny trunk makes the fruit hard to harvest, but breeders are now developing spineless varieties.

• Sea buckthorn: Thanks to specialized bacteria in its roots, sea buckthorn uses nitrogen from the air as fertilizer. These dense roots are also used to prevent soil erosion in China.

New ideas are the lifeblood of progress. Some succeed in the real world and are useful, while others fail and fall by the wayside. There is no more efficient method for utilizing the critical resources of time and money than through a system where good ideas are often well rewarded and poor ideas are less so. And there is no better way to stimulate the development of new ideas that can change the course of humanity than within the free market system. It is there that controlled risks are taken, so that if the threats to human life cannot be eliminated they at least can be greatly reduced. Governments generally lack the incentive to work quickly and efficiently, and many traditional businesses seemingly have no financial reward for acting in a benevolent manner, but businesses that are organized with benevolent goals and paired with respectable profit incentives that are reflective of the good they do are the next great evolution in business.

The challenge to us as a people, a planet....and to us as individuals, every one of us, is to identify that problem, that inefficiency that causes pain, and then find a solution that resolves that pain and results in a solution not just for today but for tomorrow and the day after that.

So look at technology and science, at math and language and art. Look at everything you can in the world, and then look inside and above. Never limit your thinking or your expectations. The solution is there. Create products, and design systems, but never forget that the magic ingredient is always people. The world's most dire problems have not been resolved for centuries through traditional measures. The world is definitely ready for something a bit more radical.

For more information and access to resources, visit our website at
www.radicalresponsebook.com